Xtreme Talk

Xtreme Talk

by
Eastman Curtis

Harrison House
Tulsa, Oklahoma

Direct quotations from the Bible appear in bold type.

2nd Printing

Xtreme Talk
ISBN 1-57794-019-9

P. O. Box 470290
Tulsa, Oklahoma 74147

Published by Harrison House
P. O. Box 35035
Tulsa, Oklahoma 74153

day
1

how do I know what God wants for me to do with my life?

First of all, when God is your focus, He blesses you with the opportunity to see the desires of your heart come to pass. Secondly, and most people always forget this part, God Himself has placed natural gifts, talents and interests in you for a reason.

For instance, why do you like music, football or debate? Because God created and ignited those desires inside of you. He placed those desires in your heart to help fulfill His plan for your life.

Delight yourself in the Lord and he will give you the desires of your heart. Commit your way to the Lord; trust in him and he will do this: He will make your righteousness shine like the dawn, the justice of your cause like the noonday sun. — Psalm 37:4-6 NIV

So how do you know what God wants you to do with your life? Look at *your* greatest desires and interests. Are they the kind of desires that would be pleasing to God? If so, then He is the One Who placed those dreams in your heart. They are there for a reason; God expects you to act on the desires He has ignited within you and trust Him to bring them to pass in your life.

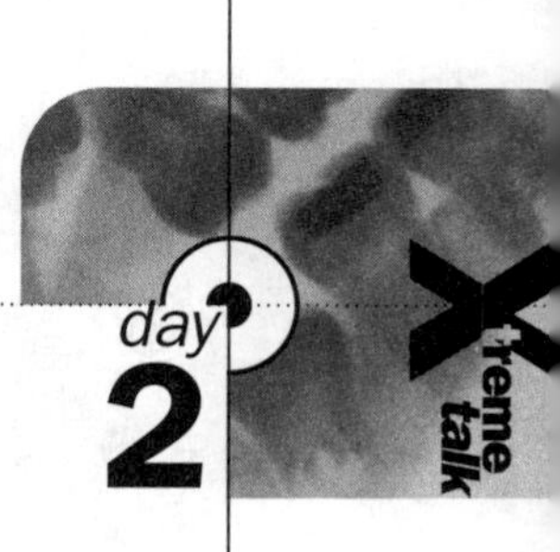

how do I accomplish my dreams?

To have a vision basically means to visualize a goal. Once you realize what it is God wants you to reach for, you need to take some important steps to make your vision come to pass.

In fact, Habakkuk 2:2-3 gives us these three essential steps to take:

1. Write the vision or goal down. Make it specific and detailed. State exactly what you intend to do.
2. Be a herald of your vision. That means that you should proclaim it to others. Of course, some people will think you are crazy, but tell it anyway.
3. Run with your vision. Don't walk, don't jog – run! Do something to move in the direction you want to go, even if it is just for the time being.

Then the Lord replied: "Write down the revelation and make it plain on tablets so that a herald may run with it. For the revelation awaits an appointed time; it speaks of the end and will not prove false. Though it linger, wait for it; it will certainly come and will not delay."
— Habakkuk 2:2,3 **NIV**

These steps sound simple, and they are. All you have to do to accomplish the dream God has planted in your heart is to *act on* it: write the vision down, speak it out — and then run with it!

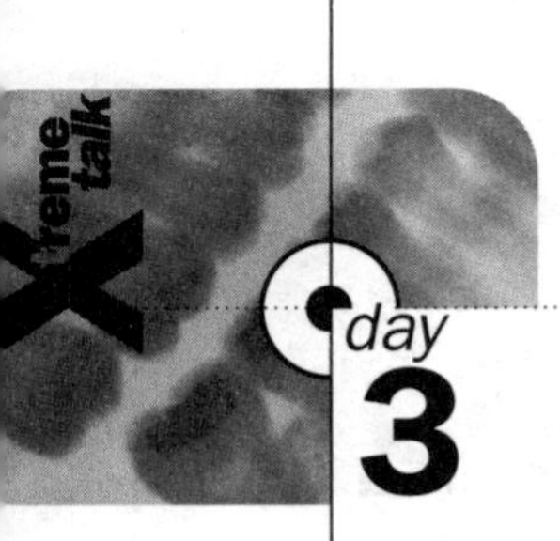

how can I stop procrastinating?

You may think procrastination is your problem, but it isn't. The problem is that you lack vision. Proverbs 29:18 (NIV) says that when there is no vision, people cast off restraint. In other words, they run wild and have no discipline.

Now check out this example: A guy at school looks horrible, and he smells worse. You know the type. All of a sudden, this same guy runs into a UFO — an "unidentified female object."

Well, pretty soon, he starts taking a little bit more time to get ready in the morning in the hope that he will run into that fascinating creature again. He rarely used deodorant before, but now he is rolling it on with gusto. A day ago, you would have wondered if he knew how to unscrew the cap to his shampoo bottle, but now you see concrete evidence that he has finally figured it out.

What happened? That young man got a vision for what he could have, and the discipline he needed to get it soon followed!

Where there is no revelation [or vision], ***the people cast off restraint; but blessed is he who keeps the law. — Proverbs 29:18 NIV***

Do you see what I mean? You aren't dealing with a discipline problem that causes you to procrastinate as much as you are dealing with a "lack of vision" problem. Once you get a vision of what you want to accomplish, the discipline to carry it out will always follow.

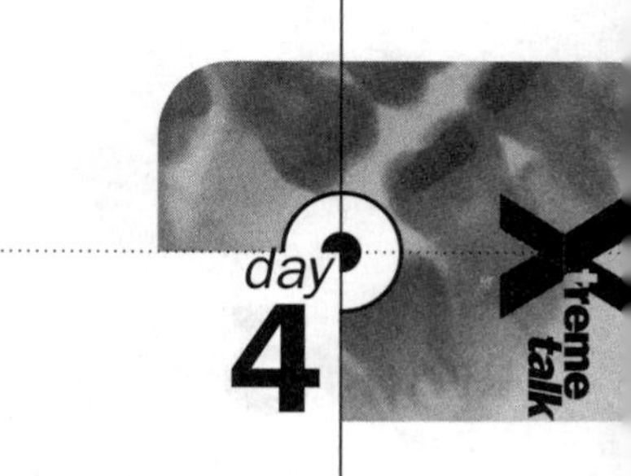

how do I find that perfect job?

First of all, there is no perfect job. They all have their ups and downs. What you want isn't "the perfect job," but the job that will best fit your ability, interests and personality. The great news is that God has already made these important decisions about your career for you.

All you need to do is pray and ask God to help you make the day-by-day decisions that will eventually get you where you know He wants you to be. Then listen to the Holy Spirit and follow through on whatever He nudges you to do that day. In the meantime, be faithful right *where you are* because God will probably use where you are to prepare you for *where you are going.*

Let's say, for example, that you know God wants you to be an engineer. It's a desire He has placed in your heart. Well, don't wait until you graduate to start testing out and acting on that desire. See if you can get a job at your level in the field, even if it means becoming an errand boy at an engineering firm. As you work at that job, you will start to find out whether or not you really like the engineering field and how you may fit in.

If engineering does seems to fit you, find out what is required to qualify for the job you envision. If you find out that you must attend college, start doing your part right now to eventually get there. Work hard while you are still in high school. Don't wait until you graduate to figure out how to study. Learning to study is a part of your responsibility *now.*

Another part of your responsibility is to be decisive. Don't waste time fooling around with the small details. Step out and do what you know you need to do — prepare your resume, fill out job applications and contact key people.

Trust in the Lord with all your heart and lean not on your own understanding; in all your ways acknowledge him, and he will make your paths straight. — Proverbs 3:5,6 NIV

After you have done all you know to do, then let go and let God do the rest because you can't force or make things happen. God knows what needs to happen to make your desire a reality, and He will take care of the rest.

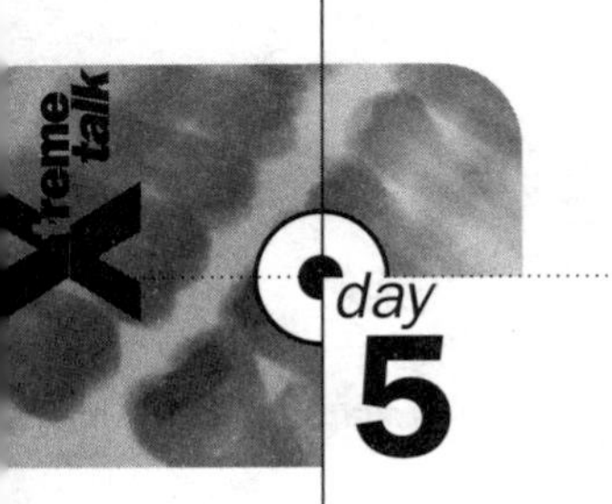

why doesn't anything seem to be happening in my life?

The farmer doesn't harvest the crop he wants when the weather is bad, when the crop isn't planted or when the soil isn't watered. God handles the seasons and the weather, but the farmer has to plant and water the seed.

So the question you have to ask yourself is this: *Have I done all I can to make sure the soil of my heart is fertile and watered?*

If not, you need to become active about tending to your "field of dreams." Plant deep in your heart those ideas and desires that God gives you, and water them by the Word. Then make sure you regularly pull out the weeds of doubt and discouragement.

So let's not allow ourselves to get fatigued doing good. At the right time we will harvest a good crop if we don't give up, or quit. Right now, therefore, every time we get the chance, let us work for the benefit of all, starting with the people closest to us in the community of faith.
— Galatians 6:9,10 THE MESSAGE

If you are doing all these things and still nothing seems to be happening, you can rest in the knowledge that God's timeline is better than yours. In the meantime, don't give up on your dreams. Your harvest will eventually come. It may not come as quickly as you had hoped, but it will most certainly come. God is faithful, and, at the right time, He will give the increase.

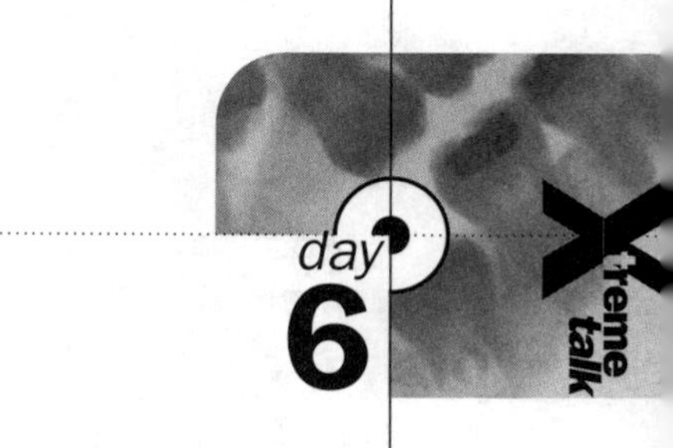

where does the Bible say I can't smoke?

If you look at the Bible as a whole, you will see a theme running through every page and every chapter: God's freedom has been made available to every man. So it isn't really an issue of cigarettes (or anorexia, anger, sexual immorality, etc.). It is a matter of choosing freedom or bondage.

Jesus came to this earth to set us free from bondage. He is the Author and Source of our freedom; He even gave His life for it. So when we choose bondage over freedom, can you imagine what an insult that is to Him?

Just because something is technically legal doesn't mean that it's spiritually appropriate. If I went around doing whatever I thought I could get by with, I'd be a slave to my whims.
— 1 Corinthians 6:12 **THE MESSAGE**

Now, smoking may not send you to hell, but bondage by choice will certainly put you on the road that leads to destruction. Don't give an inch to the devil with your freedom because he always takes a mile.

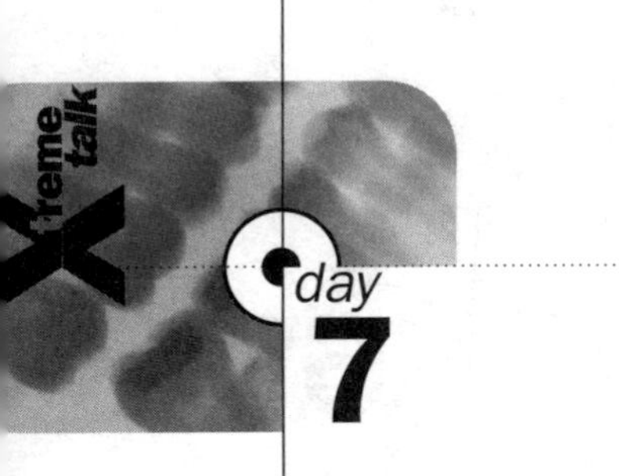

is it all right to go to parties just to have fun?

Going to parties isn't going to do any harm to you physically as long as you don't drink or take drugs. But consider this: God calls you to come out and be separate from the world so others can recognize that you are different and know that you are a Christian.

When you go to the same parties everybody else does, it cancels out that separation. Sure, you may not drink or do drugs. But as far as the other kids know, you are just a good person with good morals.

Secondly, when you spend time in an atmosphere of sin and compromise, you begin to get used to it. At first, it really hits you wrong, but after a while you become desensitized to what is going on.

Before you realize it, you find yourself justifying the compromise in your mind. Eventually you become trapped in that compromising behavior yourself, feeling like you can't get out. Once you get to that point, you are in danger of falling into nothing less than horrible bondage.

But you are the ones chosen by God, chosen for the high calling of priestly work, chosen to be a holy people, God's instruments to do his work and speak out for him, to tell others of the night-and-day difference he made for you — from nothing to something, from rejected to accepted. — 1 Peter 2:9,10 THE MESSAGE

Finally, I have one big question you need to ask yourself: *Would Jesus go?*

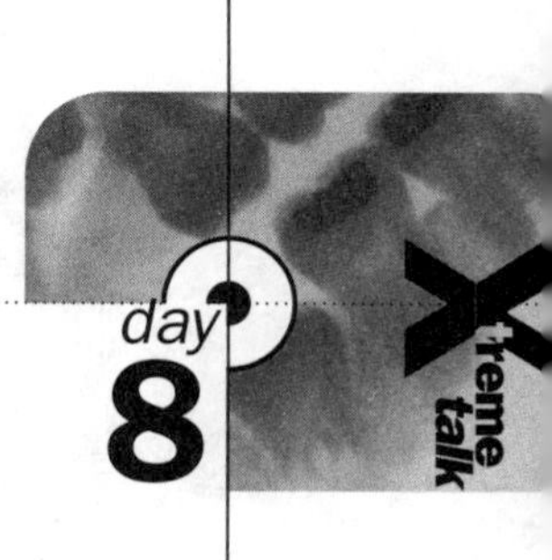

does the Bible say it is wrong to drink or to smoke marijuana?

The Bible as a whole tells a story about a God Who wants His people to be set free from death and anything that causes death. Marijuana (or pot) and alcohol are two things the world offers us as a temporary escape.

God wants you to be free of everything that pollutes your spirit and body, including pot and alcohol. Once you realize that fact, it is easy to wise up to the devil's deception and refuse to fall for it.

Don't compromise your freedom for a cheap escape. Compromise is like tooth decay. You don't feel it at first. But if you don't deal with the problem, the day will come when your whole mouth is rotted out. At that point, the slightest pressure applied to your teeth can make them begin to crumble.

From now on, think of it this way: Sin speaks a dead language that means nothing to you; God speaks your mother tongue, and you hang on every word. You are dead to sin and alive to God. That's what Jesus did.

That means you must not give sin a vote in the way you conduct your lives. Don't give it the time of day. Don't even run little errands that are connected with that old way of life. Throw yourselves wholeheartedly and full-time — remember, you've been raised from the dead! — into God's way of doing things. Sin can't tell you how to live. After all, you're not living under that old tyranny any longer. You're living in the freedom of God.
— Romans 6:11-14 THE MESSAGE

That's what compromise does. If you fall into sin and don't repent of it, that sin can eventually cause everything good in your life to crumble.

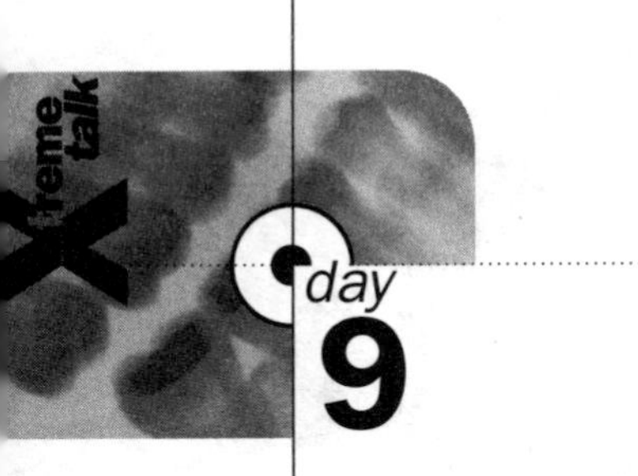

how can I make wise choices?

I just thank God for young adults who want to make wise choices. Unfortunately, many have good intentions but never follow through because of peer pressure and temptation.

However, you can take a few simple steps to increase the likelihood that you will make wise choices. First of all, only hang around good influences. Don't make temptation and peer pressure stronger forces than they already are.

Also, stay away from those who say one thing and then do another. People like that are liars and likely to get you into trouble.

***For wisdom will enter your heart, and knowledge will be pleasant to your soul. Discretion will protect you, and understanding will guard you. Wisdom will save you from the ways of wicked men, from men whose words are perverse, who leave the straight paths to walk in dark ways, who delight in doing wrong and rejoice in the perverseness of evil, whose paths are crooked and who are devious in their ways. — Proverbs 2:10-15* NIV**

Then finally — and this is so important — make your decisions before you get into tempting situations. Make it known that you don't drink and that you don't go to parties. Then it will be a whole lot easier to turn down those invitations if they come. Remember, *the decisions of tomorrow are made with the heart today.*

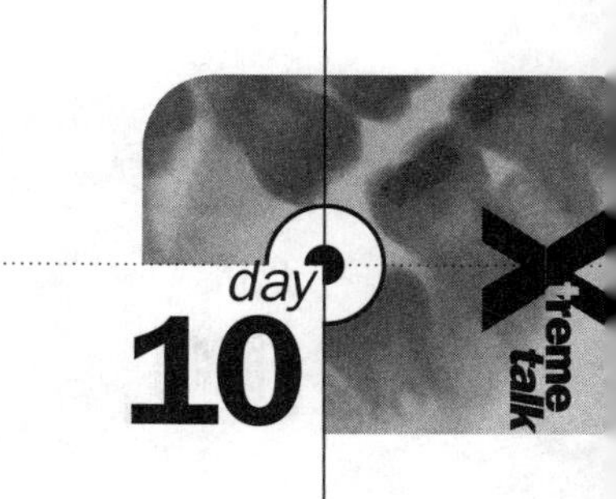

how can I be a better example of a Christian?

Just the fact that you are a Christian means your light can't be hidden unless *you* decide to hide it. That's why you should want to set a good example by staying away from drugs and alcohol.

At the same time, it is just as important that you are loving and kind toward those people who do drink and use drugs. They need to know that you care about them so they can turn to you when they need help. And believe me, they *will* need help!

Get the word out. Teach all these things. And don't let anyone put you down because you're young. Teach believers with your life: by word, by demeanor, by love, by faith, by integrity. Stay at your post reading Scripture, giving counsel, teaching. And that special gift of ministry you were given when the leaders of the church laid hands on you and prayed — keep that dusted off and in use. — 1 Timothy 4:11-14 **THE MESSAGE**

Other than that, just choose to "shine your light." Don't allow yourself to get caught up in compromising situations; instead, take a bold stand against what you know is wrong. When you do, you will be an encouragement to others who also want to do what is right.

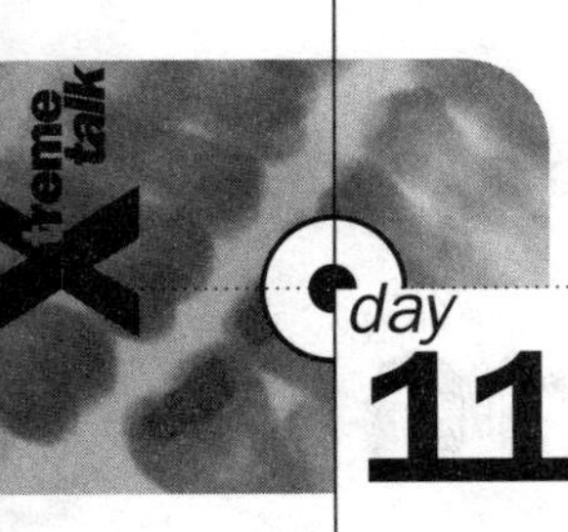

is it okay to date uncommitted Christians?

First of all, let's get one thing straight. The only kind of Christian to date is a committed one. When you date an uncommitted Christian, you are taking the risk that he or she isn't a Christian at all. And a Christian dating a non-Christian is like a fish dating a rabbit.

Sure, your date may "hop on down to the lake and take a drink once in a while." In other words, he or she may attend church. But that person can't really "dive into the water and swim." No one can live a Christian life by the power of God until his or her spiritual nature changes.

You, on the other hand, may wind up trying to live in both worlds but failing to live successfully in either. Instead of swimming freely under the water as you were created to do, you may find yourself flopping around on the dry land of worldly temptations as the air chokes you.

Don't become partners with those who reject God. How can you make a partnership out of right and wrong? That's not partnership; that's war. Is light best friends with dark? Does Christ go strolling with the Devil? Do trust and mistrust hold hands? Who would think of setting up pagan idols in God's holy Temple? But that is exactly what we are, each of us a temple in whom God lives. — 2 Corinthians 6:14-16 THE MESSAGE

Wouldn't it be much better to find someone with whom you can explore the deeps — someone who knows Jesus the way you do?

Don't risk trying to satisfy the powerful needs you have for love and acceptance with someone who can't point you to the Ultimate Source, Jesus Christ. Date Christians, and save yourself the agony of gasping for air on dry ground.

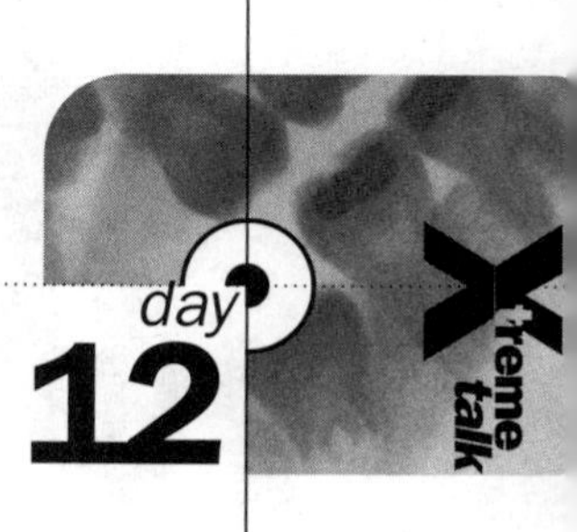

how can I find the perfect mate?

The way to find a lifetime mate who meets high standards is to set those same high standards for yourself. In other words, if you want to make sure you find the right mate in life, you must work on *becoming* the right mate.

Take the time now to develop the qualities that will make you a good spouse one day. No amount of desperate searching for someone to fulfill you will do anything to develop you spiritually.

"But I've gotta find the right guy!" you may say.

Well, even if you do accidentally bump into your ideal mate along the way, that person may fail to see in you the ideal mate he or she is looking for. If you waste your time *looking* instead of *becoming,* you won't be ready.

Stay clear of silly stories that get dressed up as religion. Exercise daily in God — no spiritual flabbiness, please! Workouts in the gymnasium are useful, but a disciplined life in God is far more so, making you fit both today and forever. You can count on this. Take it to heart. This is why we've thrown ourselves into this venture so totally. We're banking on the living God, Savior of all men and women, especially believers.
— 1 Timothy 4:7-10 **THE MESSAGE**

That's why you need to put your effort into developing yourself and your relationship with Jesus instead of just looking for someone else to be your priority. Make sure that you are always growing in the Lord. Then in God's own timing, He will bring someone across your path who has done the same.

day

13

what are God's standards about kissing, sex, etc.?

First of all, the Bible makes it very clear: Sex is an incredible gift from God reserved for the husband and wife in the covenant of marriage. God actually tells us to *flee* from situations and behavior that would tempt us to have sex with someone outside of marriage. (1 Corinthians 6:18.)

But to learn more about God's standards of physical conduct in dating, the best thing you can do is develop your personal relationship with Him. Then as you learn to let the Holy Spirit lead you in every situation, you will find yourself wanting to do the things God desires you to do. You will know the answer in your heart when you ask yourself, *Would it please God if I did such-and-such?*

One practical thing you can do to live by God's standards in dating is to draw boundary lines for yourself *before* you ever hold that person's hand. Make godly decisions to live by before you find yourself in uncomfortable situations where you have to act on those decisions.

God himself put it this way: "'I'll live in them, move into them; I'll be their God and they'll be my people. So leave the corruption and compromise; leave it for good,' says God. 'Don't link up with those who will pollute you. I want you all for myself. I'll be a Father to you; you'll be sons and daughters to me.' The Word of the Master, God."

With promises like this to pull us on, dear friends, let's make a clean break with everything that defiles or distracts us, both within and without. Let's make our entire lives fit and holy temples for the worship of God. — 2 Corinthians 6:16-18; 7:1 THE MESSAGE

You see, a person of wisdom charts his course from the beginning and avoids those cliff edges altogether. On the other hand, a fool travels as close as he can to the edge and wonders, How far is too far?

what does it mean to fall in love?

You don't *fall* into love; you *grow* into it. You fall into either lust or infatuation. The Bible defines true love as being patient, kind and unselfish. It is the kind of love that never fails.

Yes, you are human, and you may blow it every now and then. But ask yourself this: *Does the love of God shine through me enough not only to overlook the mistakes of others, but also to cause others to want to overlook my mistakes?*

That's how powerful true love really is. Falling in love — or, actually, *growing* in love — means that we understand the responsibility of loving unconditionally without fail.

Love never gives up. Love cares more for others than for self. Love doesn't want what it doesn't have. Love doesn't strut, doesn't have a swelled head, doesn't force itself on others, isn't always "me first," doesn't fly off the handle, doesn't keep score of the sins of others, doesn't revel when others grovel, takes pleasure in the flowering of truth, puts up with anything, trusts God always, always looks for the best, never looks back, but keeps going to the end.
— 1 Corinthians 13:4-7 **THE MESSAGE**

I wonder how many who feel like they are *in love* are willing to measure their relationship against this definition of love in First Corinthians?

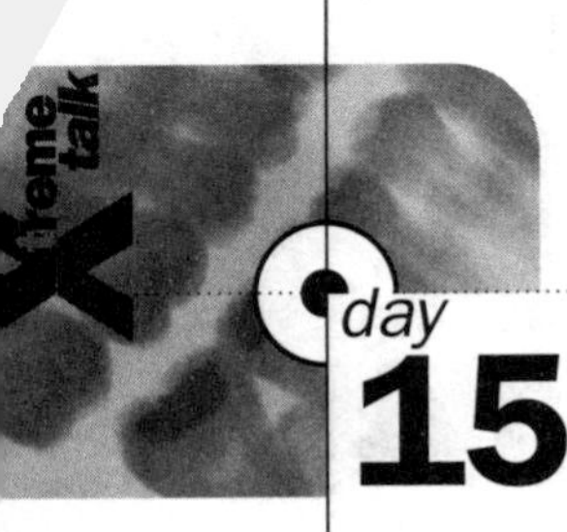

day

15

'safe sex' or 'saved sex'?

Unlike so-called "safe sex," saving sex for marriage isn't just to prevent pregnancy. It is to protect your heart from being broken. Sex was made by God to be enjoyed in the context of a covenant marriage relationship. When it is misused outside of marriage, things just won't work out right.

One of the best things you can do today for your future marriage is decide to stay faithful for your future spouse. That means you pledge to reserve your body for your mate alone *before* marriage as well as *during* marriage.

God gave us sex with guidelines because He knows we need His guidance in this area. He knows that if we misuse sex, we inevitably heap destruction upon ourselves. We may not see the negative effects of our disobedience right away, but over a period of time the harvest of destruction in our lives will become evident.

There's more to sex than mere skin on skin. Sex is as much spiritual mystery as physical fact. As written in Scripture, "The two become one." Since we want to become spiritually one with the Master, we must not pursue the kind of sex that avoids commitment and intimacy, leaving us more lonely than ever — the kind of sex that can never "become one."

There is a sense in which sexual sins are different from all others. In sexual sin we violate the sacredness of our own bodies, these bodies that were made for God-given and God-modeled love, for "becoming one" with another. Or didn't you realize that your body is a sacred place, the place of the Holy Spirit?

Don't you see that you can't live however you please, squandering what God paid such a high price for? The physical part of you is not some piece of property belonging to the spiritual part of you. God owns the whole works. So let people see God in and through your body. — 1 Corinthians 6:16-20 **THE MESSAGE**

God only wants the best for that covenant relationship you will one day enjoy with your mate. So follow His guidelines, and save sex for marriage.

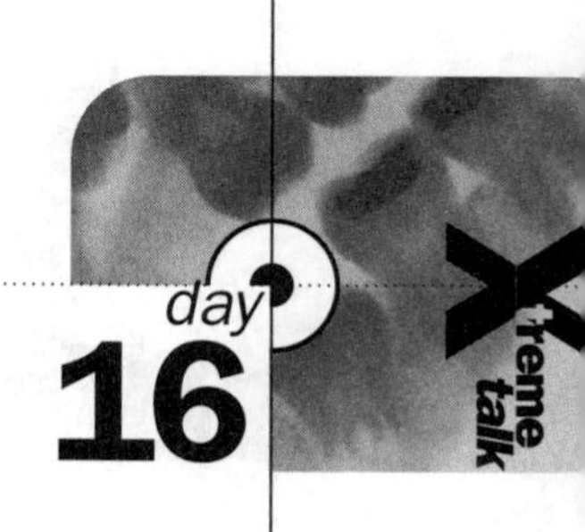

don't I need to look good in front of people?

Almost everyone worries about how they look at one time or another, especially teenagers. It is only natural. But is it really necessary? The truth is, no.

You see, God only sees something beautiful when He looks at you. Do you want to know why? Because you are made in His image. He views you as He views Himself because your heart was given back to Him when you became a Christian. And when others see Christ living in your heart, they will see that beauty too.

Cultivate inner beauty, the gentle, gracious kind that God delights in. The holy women of old were beautiful before God that way, and were good, loyal wives to their husbands. Sarah, for instance, taking care of Abraham, would address him as "my dear husband." You'll be true daughters of Sarah if you do the same, unanxious and unintimidated.
— 1 Peter 3:3-6 THE MESSAGE

There is only so much you can do about the way you look on the outside, but there is *a lot* you can do about the way your heart looks on the inside. So take the time to cultivate your relationship with Jesus. Soon His beauty will be shining through *you!*

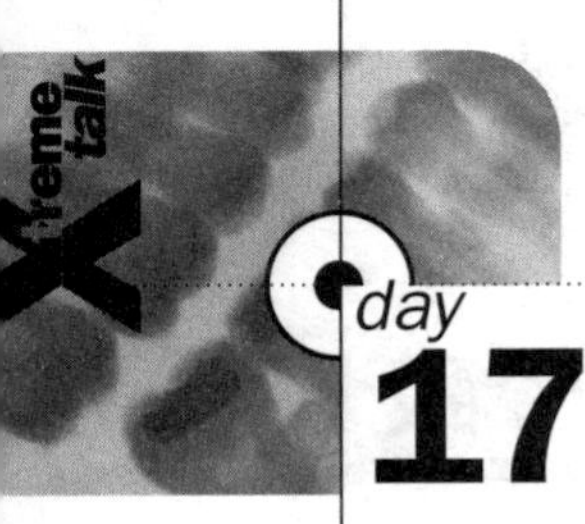

day
17

what is wrong with comparing myself to my friends?

Something that seems as innocent as comparison can sometimes grow into an ugly monster of jealousy overnight. It is just one trick weapon that the devil uses to destroy us.

When we first compare ourselves to others, we may feel as if we are doing pretty well and are somewhere near "the top of the stack." But eventually we come to realize that we may not be quite as good as someone else in a particular area. We begin to feel as if we are closer to the bottom of the stack than we realized. Slowly, our character is poisoned with envy. Soon we become so infected with that poison, it's hard to remember what we even liked about ourselves to begin with.

Sure, there may be someone who does some things better in the natural than you do. But that's okay. You just need to accept that fact and realize that God has given you special gifts and talents as well, even though they may be in totally different areas.

But if you harbor bitter envy and selfish ambition in your hearts, do not boast about it or deny the truth. Such "wisdom" does not come down from heaven but is earthly, unspiritual, of the devil. For where you have envy and selfish ambition, there you find disorder and every evil practice. — James 3:14-16 NIV

So find out what your particular gifts are and focus in on them. Allow Christ to develop you into the unique person that He created you to be. Once you realize that Jesus has already purchased and given to you every good thing you could ever need to accomplish what He has called you to do, you won't be so tempted to drink the poisonous wine of jealousy.

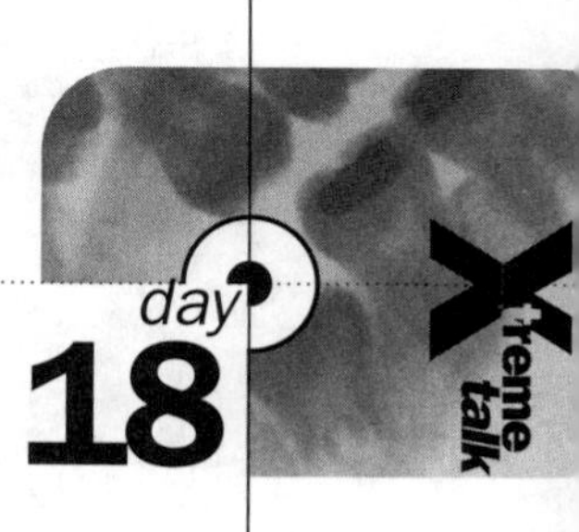

why do people think I am stuck up?

Sometimes we come across to others as being stuck up or conceited because deep down inside we are insecure about who we really are; therefore, we try to be someone we are *not.* We are afraid that if people really knew who we were, they wouldn't like us. So we keep them at arm's length, erecting a big, invisible wall with a sign posted that says, "I don't want you to really know me, so this is the person I am pretending to be."

Sometimes people interpret that type of behavior as pride. But, in reality, it is a problem of low self-esteem.

A lack of self-esteem can ruin your relationships because it causes you to constantly put up walls. People are only able to have a relationship with "the pretend you" while you hide "the real you" inside.

I praise you because I am fearfully and wonderfully made; your works are wonderful, I know that full well. — Psalm 139:14 NIV

So what do you need to do? Just refuse to build that wall. Instead, find out what God thinks about you. Spend time in the Word building up your self-esteem.

how can I get out of self-pity and do something for God's kingdom?

You know, it is so true that self-pity is from the devil. When you are busy looking at your own bellybutton, you have no clue about what God is doing right in front of your eyes!

We need to embrace God's remedy for self-pity, which is to *let go of the past.* Holding on to past hurts and failures keeps us from receiving the blessings that lie ahead of us. God designs those future blessings to lift us above the hurtful situations of the past in order to bring healing.

Whining and complaining will only make you more upset about your situation. God has called you to be an overcomer *over* your circumstances.

I'm not saying that I have this all together, that I have it made. But I am well on my way, reaching out for Christ, who has so wondrously reached out for me. Friends, don't get me wrong: By no means do I count myself an expert in all of this, but I've got my eye on the goal, where God is beckoning us onward — to Jesus. I'm off and running, and I'm not turning back.

So let's keep focused on that goal, those of us who want everything God has for us. If any of you have something else in mind, something less than total commitment, God will clear your blurred vision — you'll see it yet! Now that we're on the right track, let's stay on it.

— Philippians 3:12-16 THE MESSAGE

Now, the devil knows that if he can keep you selfishly focused on your own hurts, he will keep you from doing what God wants you to do and therefore rob you of the blessing God has for you. So if you really want to foil the enemy's plans for you and get out of self-pity, follow this word of advice: Focus on what God is doing in your life and refuse to embrace the lies of the devil.

how do I get my feelings in line with God?

You know, even though it seems as if our feelings make up who we are, they are really only second place to the Word of God inside of us.

You see, our feelings change every day. So if we allow ourselves to be led by our emotions or by what others think of us, our own sense of identity will also change every day.

On the other hand, when our identity is based on what God says or thinks about us, then He changes us day by day into the person He already sees. Just like an uncut diamond that is carefully chipped at until its real beauty is revealed, we are being wonderfully made into the image of Christ.

But we have to cooperate with God by choosing to live by a greater standard than our own feelings and other people's opinions — the standard of God's Word.

***Dear friends, now we are children of God, and what we will be has not yet been made known. But we know that when he appears, we shall be like him, for we shall see him as he is. Everyone who has this hope in him purifies himself, just as he is pure. — 1 John 3:2,3* NIV**

Jesus Christ died so we could live and be identified with Him. But the only way we will ever get our feelings to line up with our true identity in Him is to constantly feed on the Word of God.

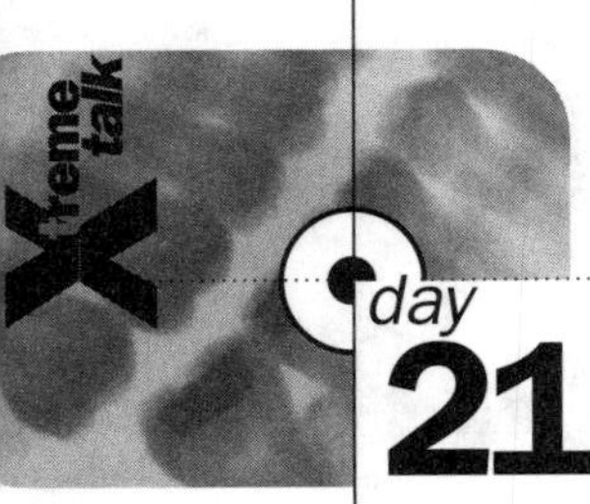

how do I grow spiritually?

Spiritual growth simply means that you are gaining more and more understanding about spiritual things, which causes you to walk closer to God in every part of your life.

You have a spirit man that can be instantly born again. However, your born-again spirit still needs to be taught and fed just like a baby does.

Besides digging into the Word, the best way to grow spiritually is to pray. You see, the more time you spend with a person, the better you get to know and understand that person. It's the same way in your relationship with God. You can't build a *relationship* if you don't take time for *fellowship.*

You know, my wife and I got so excited when our little boy first started talking, even though we couldn't understand the words he was saying. But then as he learned to communicate more and more in the same language, we began to understand each other perfectly. (Well, almost!)

The same thing happens when you start praying to God. At first, you may not hear His voice very well or understand what He is saying to you. But the more you fellowship with Him, the easier it becomes to hear Him and respond to His voice.

I have a lot more to say about this, but it is hard to get it across to you since you've picked up this bad habit of not listening. By this time you ought to be teachers yourselves, yet here I find you need someone to sit down with you and go over the basics on God again, starting from square one — baby's milk, when you should have been on solid food long ago! Milk is for beginners, inexperienced in God's ways; solid food is for the mature, who have some practice in telling right from wrong.
— Hebrews 5:11-14 THE MESSAGE

So work on growing spiritually through the Word and through prayer. As you do, you will learn how to grab hold of the blessings God has for you, thanking Him continually for abundant provision in every area of life!

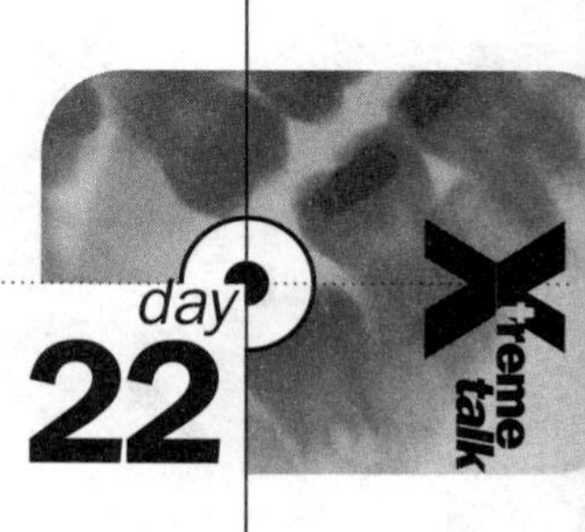

how can I understand the love of God?

I believe the best way to understand the love of God is to read His sixty-six books of love letters to you – all included in the Bible. Love is one of the most, if not *the* most, used words in the Bible. It must be important to God!

Here's some practical things to help you get into the Bible: First, find a good translation in common English. Next, begin to read a book of the Bible that interests you. Most probably it won't be Leviticus! The Gospels of Matthew, Mark, Luke and John are great places to learn more about Christ's love for you personally.

Do you think anyone is going to be able to drive a wedge between us and Christ's love for us? There is no way! Not trouble, not hard times, not hatred, not hunger, not homelessness, not bullying threats, not backstabbing, not even the worst sins listed in Scripture.
— Romans 8:35 **THE MESSAGE**

God loves you so much that He wants to make His love crystal clear to you. Therefore, He rewrites His love letter to you with enthusiasm and zeal every day that you take time to read it!

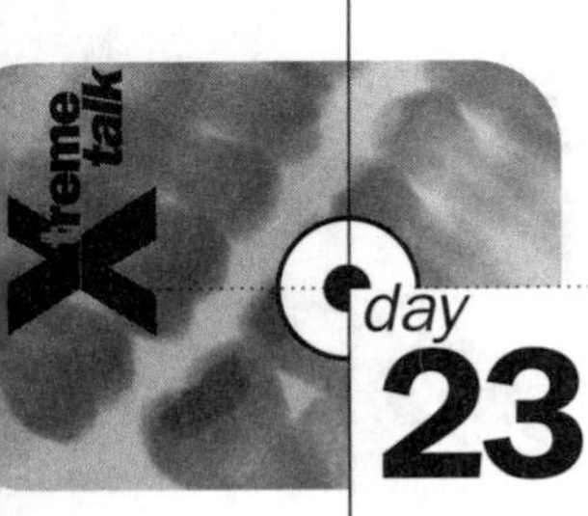

how do I find a church?

A church is meant to encourage you. It is a place where you can be strengthened and instructed in the things of God.

You see, when you are born again, you are like an infant in many ways. In the natural, we know how dangerous it would be for a little baby to crawl off into the woods and try to raise himself. It isn't possible. The baby just wouldn't survive!

Well, that is exactly what it would be like for you if you don't find a good church home; you wouldn't survive in your walk with God. So if you and your family don't already attend church together, find a church home for yourself where you can attend regularly and belong — a place where you can get to know the people and they can get to know you.

Visit a few different churches until you find one where you feel like you can grow. If you will stay hungry for God, He will see that you get spiritually fed. He will lead you to the people you need to meet and the places where you need to be.

You should look forward to going to church because it's one of your best opportunities to learn more about God. Church can be an exciting place to be as you sense the work of the Holy Spirit in your life.

So let's do it — full of belief, confident that we're presentable inside and out. Let's keep a firm grip on the promises that keep us going. He always keeps his word. Let's see how inventive we can be in encouraging love and helping out, not avoiding worshiping together as some do but spurring each other on, especially as we see the big Day approaching.
— Hebrews 10:23-25 THE MESSAGE

Just follow the Holy Spirit's direction. Go to church and pay attention. If you will do that, I guarantee that you will get something out of it!

how important is it to have godly friends?

It can be difficult to be a Christian in a non-Christian world. I think that is why the disciples really loved to spend time with each other. They were a great encouragement to one another.

In the same way, we need to have someone who can encourage us and pray with us every day. Not only is it good just to talk to someone we feel comfortable with about spiritual issues, but having someone to be accountable to really helps protect us against peer pressure and keeps our focus on a godly life.

Someone once said that people are like shoes; they don't do much for you until you have a pair. That's especially true regarding friends who are strong Christians.

***As iron sharpens iron, so one man sharpens another. — Proverbs 27:17* NIV**

So surround yourself with godly friends who will be an anchor to help keep you solid in your walk with God. Just don't allow your close relationships to become an exclusive clique that doesn't reach out to touch the lives of others in a meaningful way.

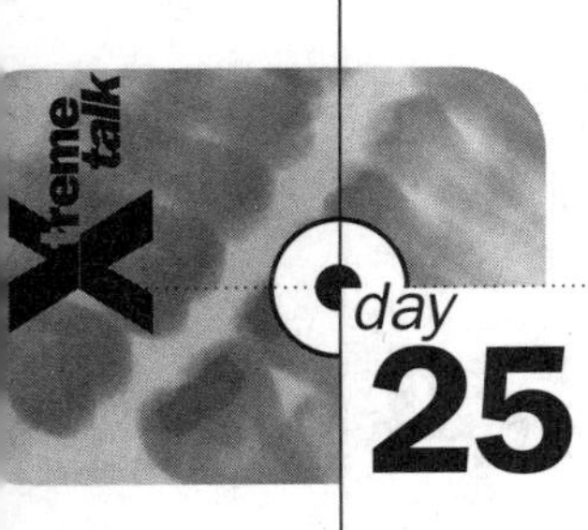

day
25

how important is acting on the Word of God?

I remember when I was a youth pastor, I saw two families get saved about the same time. But in the months and years that followed, one family grew spiritually and was blessed while the other family always seemed one step behind.

I wondered why there was such a difference between the two families' spiritual growth because God is not a respecter of persons. Both families went to the same church, and both heard the same preaching. In fact, the two sets of parents sat in the same choir. I finally came to realize what made the difference: One family just heard the Word, whereas the other one heard the Word and acted on it.

You see, it isn't enough just to study God's Word or memorize it. We have to take it one step further. We have to become *doers* of the Word.

For example, you can know that you have authority over the devil. But until you use that authority to stop the devil's attacks in your own life, you will never really experience God's best.

***Don't fool yourself into thinking that you are a listener when you are anything but, letting the Word go in one ear and out the other. Act on what you hear! Those who hear and don't act are like those who glance in the mirror, walk away, and two minutes later have no idea who they are, what they look like. — James 1:22-24* THE MESSAGE**

Do you want to be blessed in all you do? Be a doer of the Word!

how important are my grades to God?

Did you know that God is really concerned about your grades? I know that from personal experience. Before I was saved, I was a flunky in school. But after I became a Christian, I was on the honor roll every semester. Since God really helped me in this area of making good grades, I want to pass on a few things I learned to you.

First, Matthew 6:33 says that if you seek first the kingdom of God and His righteousness, all these *things* shall be added unto you. So even though you may feel pressured with your responsibilities at school, don't forget to seek God in your thought life and in your actions. Keep Him as first priority in your life, and one of the things He will add to you is good grades.

Second, start speaking what God's Word says about you. For example, First Corinthians 2:16 says that you have the mind of Christ. So say that about yourself and believe it, regardless of who has told you otherwise. This is one of those times you need to make a determination to not only hear the Word, but to act on it as well.

Steep your life in God-reality, God-initiative, God-provisions. Don't worry about missing out. You'll find all your everyday human concerns will be met. — Matthew 6:33 THE MESSAGE

Third, put your hand to your studies. When you are diligent, God will bless you. In fact, He has promised to bless whatever you set your hand to!

day
27

what is the big deal about being popular?

You may think that whether or not you are popular at school is unimportant to God. But it *is* important to Him. The Word says more than once that God wants to grant you favor with men. (Proverbs 3:3-4.)

It is evident that God does want you to enjoy favor with friends at school. But He also wants you to be an instrument of friendship.

So he went back to Nazareth with them, and lived obediently with them. His mother held these things dearly, deep within herself. And Jesus matured, growing up in both body and spirit, blessed by both God and people. — Luke 2:51,52 THE MESSAGE

God knows the best way for you to make and keep friends is to be considerate of their needs. So determine what some of your own interests are. Then find other people at school with similar interests and take the first steps toward building friendships with them. God will be faithful to make sure that those seeds of kindness will yield a garden full of friends.

what is wrong with gossip?

The Lord wants our words to provide nourishment for others. This means that when we tell people something, we do it to benefit and encourage them.

The truth is, we all have an opportunity to gossip every day. And it doesn't matter if what we say is true or a complete lie. The point of gossip is that we are talking about someone else's life without that person being present, knowing that the information we are passing on is none of our business nor the business of the person we are talking to.

People get hurt because of gossip and rumors. In fact, how would you like it if you knew someone was talking about you the way you were talking about him or her, even if the information were true?

Since they didn't bother to acknowledge God, God quit bothering them and let them run loose. And then all hell broke loose: rampant evil, grabbing and grasping, vicious backstabbing. They made life hell on earth with their envy, wanton killing, bickering, and cheating. Look at them: mean-spirited, venomous, fork-tongued God-bashers. Bullies, swaggerers, insufferable windbags! They keep inventing new ways of wrecking lives. They ditch their parents when they get in the way. Stupid, slimy, cruel, coldblooded. And it's not as if they don't know better. They know perfectly well they're spitting in God's face. And they don't care — worse, they hand out prizes to those who do the worst things best!
— Romans 1:28-32 THE MESSAGE

You should strive to treat others the way you want to be treated. So make your words full of good nutrition and not the junk food of gossip. Junk food may taste good for a while, but as the package says — there is no nutritional value in it!

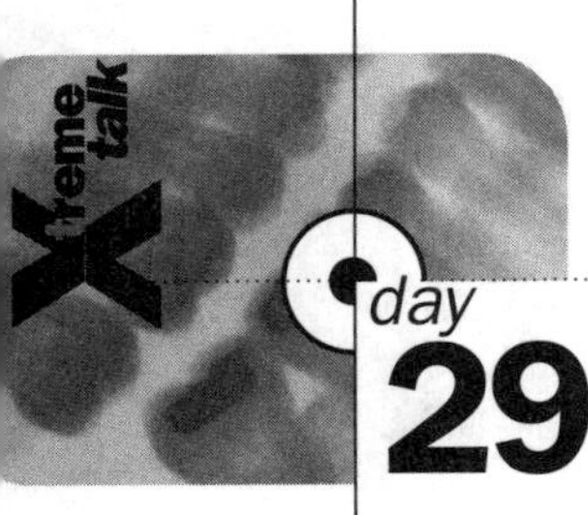

why is it important who I hang around with?

One of the hardest things about junior high and high school can be to find friends who aren't going to pressure you to do ungodly things. The best option you have is to make sure that you are hanging around people who respect your values and beliefs.

But what do you do about those who don't respect your stand for God? I know how that is. When I got saved, I was at a school full of friends who remembered me as a drinking, smoking party animal. They were really disappointed when I wouldn't party with them anymore.

But that didn't matter to me. I just turned the tables on my friends with positive peer pressure. When they cornered me and asked, "Do you really believe that stuff about God?" I always came back with, "Do you mean that you *don't?*"

When you respond that way, *you* are providing the peer pressure, not your friends. That's a much better position to be in.

But you are the ones chosen by God, chosen for the high calling of priestly work, chosen to be a holy people, God's instruments to do his work and speak out for him, to tell others of the night-and-day difference he made for you — from nothing to something, from rejected to accepted.

Friends, this world is not your home, so don't make yourselves cozy in it. Don't indulge your ego at the expense of your soul. Live an exemplary life among the natives so that your actions will refute their prejudices. Then they'll be won over to God's side and be there to join in the celebration when he arrives. — 1 Peter 2:9-12 THE MESSAGE

So trust God. He will give you the words to say to your peers when the time comes. And He will help you find friends who respect and agree with your stand for God.

does God want me to make a difference now?

It's true — God does want you to make a difference in your high school. And if you really want to make a difference, then take to heart the following five suggestions. I guarantee you that if you will do these five things, you will make a significant impact for Jesus in your high school.

1. Wear a Christian T-shirt so that everywhere you go, you will be preaching a message about Jesus.
2. Carry your Bible to every class, and read it when you have some extra time.
3. Pray over your lunch, not only because it needs to be prayed over, but because it will remind those around you of God's presence, even in the lunchroom.
4. Read one chapter of the Bible in the cafeteria.
5. Answer the questions people ask about Jesus — and I promise you, they *will* ask. When they do, be sure to brag on Him!

Use your heads as you live and work among outsiders. Don't miss a trick. Make the most of every opportunity. Be gracious in your speech. The goal is to bring out the best in others in a conversation, not put them down, not cut them out. — Colossians 4:5,6 THE MESSAGE

does God care if I live or die?

Regardless of what you face in life that could cause you to contemplate suicide, it's so important to understand that God knows and cares about how you feel.

When Jesus died, He was rejected and left alone. He went through the agony of death so you don't have to. He died so you can have the fullest life possible when you accept Him into your heart.

God desires to give you forgiveness. He wants to cleanse away all the sins in your life by the blood of Jesus and provide a way out for you. But first you have to turn to Him and allow Him to begin to work things out in your life. If you will trust Him and do what He says to do, He will bring you through the hard times and give you new hope for the future.

Christ arrives right on time to make this happen. He didn't, and doesn't, wait for us to get ready. He presented himself for this sacrificial death when we were far too weak and rebellious to do anything to get ourselves ready. And even if we hadn't been so weak, we wouldn't have known what to do anyway. We can understand someone dying for a person worth dying for, and we can understand how someone good and noble could inspire us to selfless sacrifice. But God put his love on the line for us by offering his Son in sacrificial death while we were of no use whatever to him.
— Romans 5:6-8 THE MESSAGE

God is your Father, and He cares about you. He is *for* you, not against you. He wants you to experience happiness, fulfillment, fun and adventure here in this life. But you have to start the process by trusting in Him.

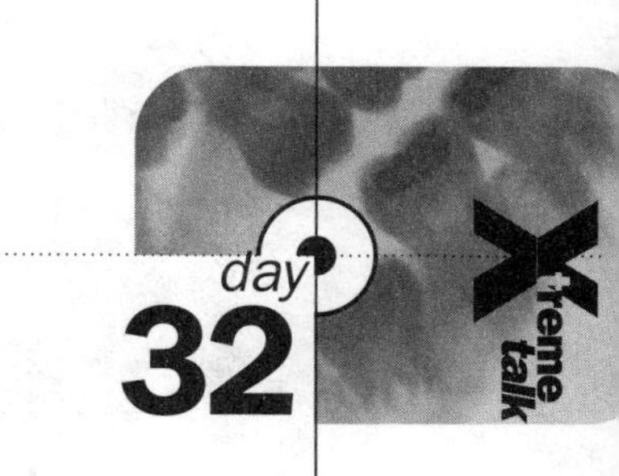

my boyfriend (or girlfriend) left me. does anyone really love me?

Sometimes we can get so caught up in our circumstances. We may think, *If one more person walks out of my life, I will be convinced beyond a shadow of a doubt that I'm the scum of the earth.*

But do you know something? You are *not* scum, no matter what anyone else does to make you feel that way. In fact, God is always right beside you, ready to comfort you. He wants to help you through every bit of loneliness you may be going through.

But in order to survive all the broken relationships that may come our way, our identity has to be in Christ. He is the only One Who will never disappoint us. He is the only One Who will never leave us, no matter what else happens in our lives.

Don't be obsessed with getting more material things. Be relaxed with what you have. Since God assured us, "I'll never let you down, never walk off and leave you," we can boldly quote, "God is there, ready to help; I'm fearless no matter what. Who or what can get to me?"
— Hebrews 13:5 THE MESSAGE

Think about this: The only One Who won't disappoint us cares about us and loves us more than we could ever imagine. So when we begin to think and feel alone and unloved, we need to hold on to what we know God says in His Word about us and not let Satan or anyone else tell us otherwise.

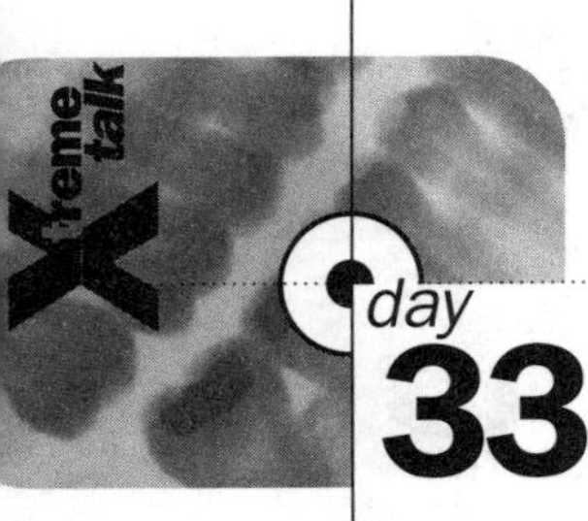

day **33**

when someone close to us dies, doesn't God care?

You know, there are a lot of things in life that happen to us that we don't understand. Death is one of them. But if we will go to God when we lose a loved one, He will help us overcome depression and fear.

If you are dealing with the death of someone you love, God wants you to *seek* Him, not to *blame* Him. Remember, He is the Giver of life, not the Giver of death.

"I'm telling you these things while I'm still living with you. The Friend, the Holy Spirit whom the Father will send at my request, will make everything plain to you. He will remind you of all the things I have told you. I'm leaving you well and whole. That's my parting gift to you. Peace. I don't leave you the way you're used to being left — feeling abandoned, bereft. So don't be upset. Don't be distraught. — John 14:25-27 **THE MESSAGE**

And even though you may never find the answer to all the questions that run through your mind, you can still turn to the Answer — Jesus Christ. In Him, you will find a peace that is greater than all your questions and strong enough to carry you through.

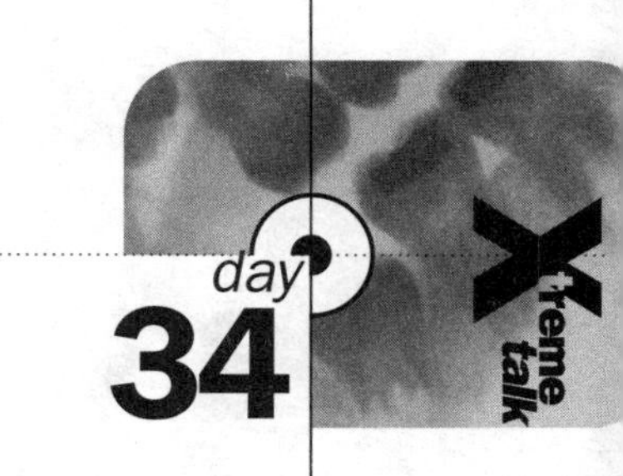

why is it so boring to be a Christian?

Probably the reason you think the Christian life is boring is that your spirit has become satisfied with the status quo instead of staying hungry for God. When you are satisfied, you become spiritually stagnant. And if you have ever seen or smelled a stagnant pond, you know what I mean when I say stagnant. It's not a pretty — or a sweet-smelling — picture!

When you are hungry for more of God, He will begin to change you, and you won't be able to stay the same for long. As a matter of fact, following God and the leading of His Spirit will often lead to a life of high adventure that you never could have expected or imagined.

Unfortunately, some people confuse religion with God. But the two are definitely *not* the same.

Religion is man-inspired and often lacks the approval and infusion of the Spirit of God. On the other hand, when God gets involved with man, there is a relationship that is dynamic, not static.

That kind of dynamic relationship with God doesn't just happen in the church, because He goes with you wherever you go. With God, anything can happen if you are open to His leading and listening to Him as you go.

Ask and it will be given to you; seek and you will find; knock and the door will be opened to you. For everyone who asks receives; he who seeks finds; and to him who knocks, the door will be opened. — Matthew 7:7,8 NIV

So get hungry for a relationship with God. Then hold on to your hat — because life won't be boring anymore!

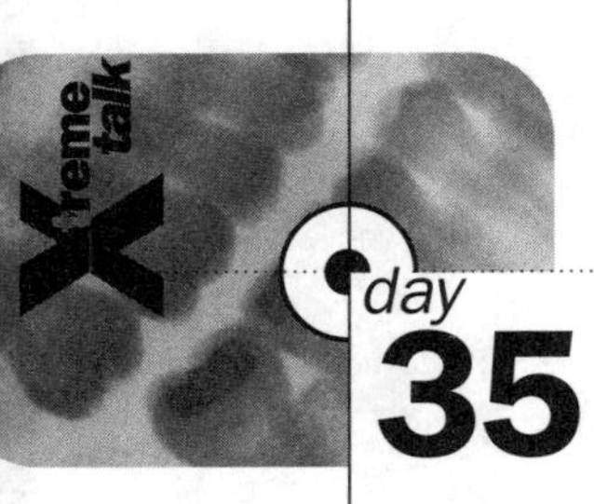

day
35

when I get rejected and depressed, how do I climb out?

God loves you more than any human ever could. That's really good to know because humans disappoint us all the time. In fact, we even disappoint ourselves. The good thing about God's love is that it is perfect. It just isn't in His character or nature to be unfaithful in His love.

When we go through feelings of rejection, the biggest ache often seems to come from loneliness. Hardly anyone cares about being rejected when they are surrounded by people who cherish and love them consistently.

You need to know that, regardless of what is happening around you, God loves you and cherishes you consistently. His desire is to see you healthy, happy and totally relying on Him for acceptance and peace.

***Since, then, we do not have the excuse of ignorance, everything — and I do mean everything — connected with that old way of life has to go. It's rotten through and through. Get rid of it! And then take on an entirely new way of life — a God-fashioned life, a life renewed from the inside and working itself into your conduct as God accurately reproduces his character in you. — Ephesians 4:22-24* THE MESSAGE**

Find out who Christ says you are in the Word. Then when a tidal wave of rejection and depression threatens your shoreline, you can surf right through it, upheld by God's love!

I survived my mom and dad's divorce, but why do I still hurt?

I get so excited when I hear young people talk about surviving a divorce. You see, I understand. I had to go through it, too, and I know it can be rough.

Do you know what many of us survivors have found to be true? God the Holy Spirit is our Comforter, no matter what we are going through.

Now, divorce does raise a lot of questions, such as, "Why did this happen?" or "What am I going to do?" But don't waste your time trying to find an answer. Turn to *the* Answer — Jesus Christ. God will turn the devil's plan around for your good and for His glory.

All praise to the God and Father of our Master, Jesus the Messiah! Father of all mercy! God of all healing counsel! He comes alongside us when we go through hard times, and before you know it, he brings us alongside someone else who is going through hard times so that we can be there for that person just as God was there for us. We have plenty of hard times that come from following the Messiah, but no more so than the good times of his healing comfort — we get a full measure of that, too.
— 2 Corinthians 1:3-5 THE MESSAGE

So let Jesus bind up your wounds. He will move in your life to heal you and help you go on to fulfill your destiny. That is what I call a permanent relationship!

if I think my parents are wrong, is it wrong for me to disrespect them?

When you disagree with your friends, you often respect their viewpoint enough to at least hear them out. Well, don't your parents deserve the same kind of respect, but even more so? Even if you don't feel that your parents deserve respect, God commands you to give it to them anyway.

Think about what a driver does when the oil light goes on in his car. He goes out and checks the oil, regardless of whether he thinks the light is accurate or not. If he does happen to be low on oil, he can add some and save himself from having to buy a new engine.

It's the same with the advice your parents may have to give to you. You may think what they have to say is unnecessary. But at least you can listen, whether or not you agree with their viewpoint. It's very possible that their advice could save you a lot of trouble if you would only heed it.

Children, do what your parents tell you. This is only right. "Honor your father and mother" is the first commandment that has a promise attached to it, namely, "so you will live well and have a long life."

Fathers, don't exasperate your children by coming down hard on them. Take them by the hand and lead them in the way of the Master.
— Ephesians 6:1-4 THE MESSAGE

Believe it or not, your parents want to understand you. They really do. And it is important that you respect them enough to try to understand them too. When you do this, you are acting on the godly principle of honoring your parents, and you will reap blessing and honor not only from your parents, but from others as well — including your friends.

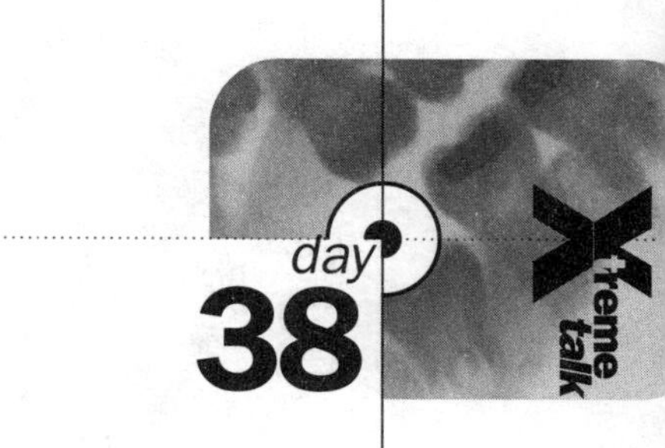

what can I do to win my dad to Jesus?

The greatest thing you can do to win your dad to Christ is to be an example of Christ's love. I am talking about unconditional, nonjudgmental love.

Also, be sure to be respectful and obedient. Try to listen to your dad and locate where he is spiritually. When he asks questions, answer him in love and not in judgment.

But mostly, show them all this by doing it yourself, incorruptible in your teaching, your words solid and sane. Then anyone who is dead set against us, when he finds nothing weird or misguided, might eventually come around. — Titus 2:7,8 THE MESSAGE

Most of all, teach your dad about Jesus not only by your words, but by the way you live. When he sees the consistency and peace in your life, your Christian walk will become contagious. Your dad will want what you have!

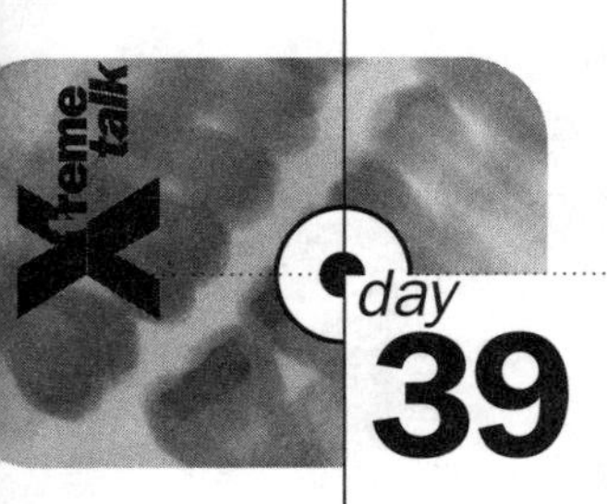

day
39

how can I get over this anger after seeing someone killed by abuse?

Wow, that's a tough question! As a father, I can't imagine anything worse than one of my kids getting hurt on purpose by somebody else.

God feels the same way — in fact, more so. Not only does He want to rescue us out of any situation like that if it is still happening, but He also wants to be our Source of comfort and healing when the memories of the abuse try to come back to torture us.

If you or someone you know is being abused, please tell someone you trust, such as a parent, pastor, youth pastor or another adult. If you have been abused in the past, know that God is your Source of comfort and that you have the liberty to seek out a godly counselor in order to talk things out.

Finally, for your own sake, ask God to help you forgive the person who hurt either you or someone you love. If you don't forgive, your bitterness will eventually hurt you more than anyone else.

***In prayer there is a connection between what God does and what you do. You can't get forgiveness from God, for instance, without also forgiving others. If you refuse to do your part, you cut yourself off from God's part.* — *Matthew 6:14,15* THE MESSAGE**

God cares about you and your hurts. He wants to help you and heal you, so draw near to Him.

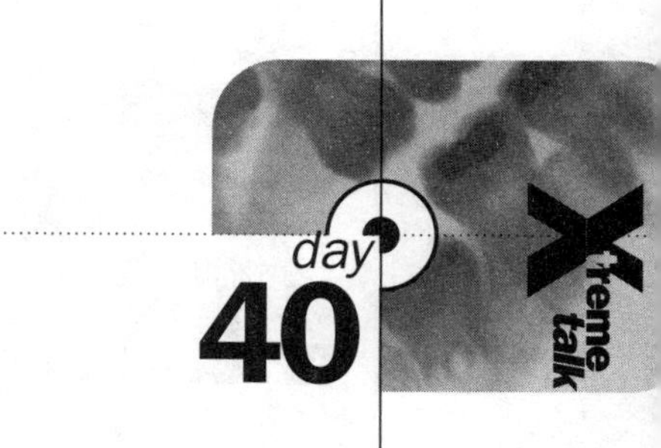

how can I get along with my stepparents?

I can tell you from experience that stepparents can be a brand-new challenge in life. In fact, I remember well the time when, right in the middle of working through all the emotions I had as a result of my parents' divorce, I had to turn around and readjust to brand-new parents.

That experience can be a stretch to your love walk, but God's love in you can prevail. Here are some things that will make it easier for you to adjust to stepparents:

First, show your stepparents respect. Real respect translates into love. I am talking about real love — active love that makes a difference. As you determine in your heart to show this kind of love, God will help develop it in you.

Second, try to remember that it is just as much a stretch for your stepparents to adjust to you as it is for you to adjust to them. It may be hard to see it from their perspective at first, but at least try to put yourself in their place and understand what they may be dealing with.

If someone claims, "I know him well!" but doesn't keep his commandments, he's obviously a liar. His life doesn't match his words. But the one who keeps God's word is the person in whom we see God's mature love. This is the only way to be sure we're in God. Anyone who claims to be intimate with God ought to live the same kind of life Jesus lived.
— 1 John 2:3-6 THE MESSAGE

With God's help and your decision to walk in love, a great relationship is bound to begin between you and your stepparents.

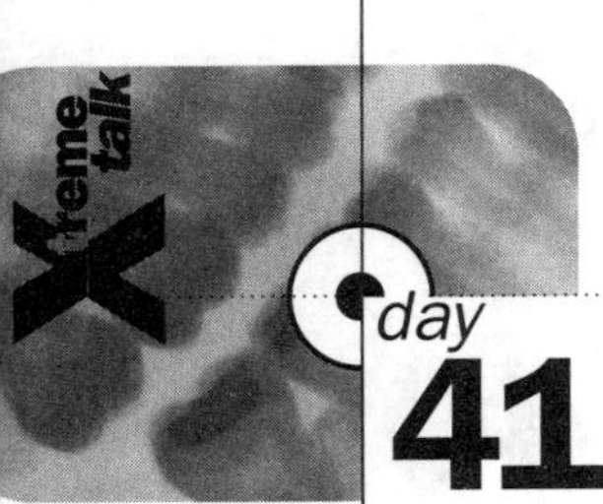

day
41

what is the matter with a few sarcastic jokes once in a while?

The Bible says in Proverbs 26:18-19 that the one who jokes cruelly and deceptively is like a madman who slings firebrands and deadly arrows. That sounds pretty serious, doesn't it?

You see, the things you say not only reflect what is in your heart, but they also affect other people's feelings. Sarcasm is just one of those bad habits that can creep into the way you talk if you aren't careful, especially if you hang around other people who are sarcastic.

A sarcastic joke may seem so innocent. After all, it's just a joke, right? But take a moment to think about how the person on the other end of that joke must feel. Words really do affect people.

***Like a madman shooting firebrands or deadly arrows is a man who deceives his neighbor and says, "I was only joking!" — Proverbs 26:18,19* NIV**

It is God's desire that we use our words to build each other up rather than tear each other down. That's why it's a good idea to steer clear of jokes that use sarcasm and insults to get a laugh.

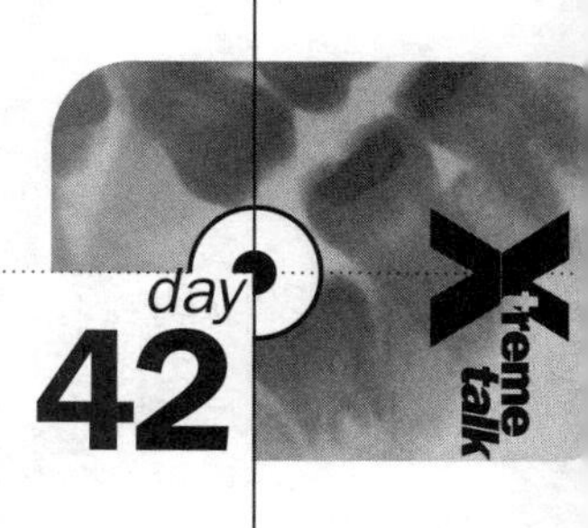

is it okay to take my time to get my responsibilities done?

As you probably already know, God can't bless laziness because He created us to find fulfillment in work. In fact, the Bible says that being lazy can cause poverty to come on us like a bandit. It is only by working as unto the Lord that we can truly enjoy every good thing He has promised.

Now, it may be *easier* for you to sit back and let someone else do the work, but it isn't *better.* And don't get caught in the trap of thinking that hard work only applies to those who are over eighteen. The character you build today as a teenager by being diligent to fulfill your responsibilities will last you the rest of your life.

A little sleep, a little slumber, a little folding of the hands to rest — and poverty will come on you like a bandit and scarcity like an armed man. — Proverbs 24:33,34 NIV

Diligence and laziness are both habits that begin early in life. So get off your hind end, and start developing the habit of diligence!

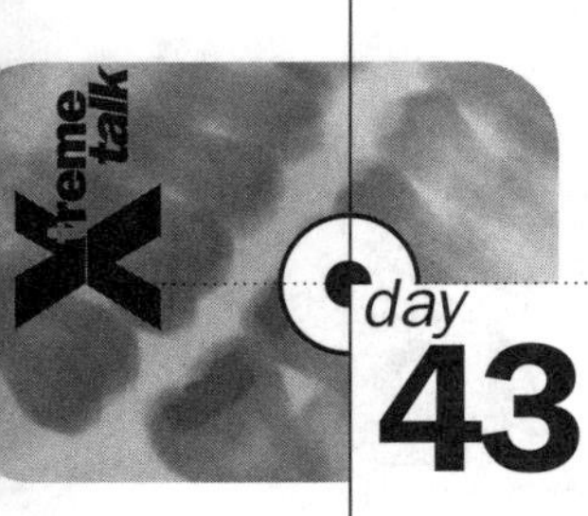

day
43

how do I get rid of an addiction that controls me?

God's Word says, **I can do all things through Christ which strengtheneth me** (Philippians 4:13). There are no ifs, ands or buts about it.

A lot of people try to get rid of their addictions, but soon they fall right back into the same old patterns. Why? Because they are trying to quit in their own strength. If they would accept Christ, however, they would no longer have to do anything in their own strength.

Let me tell you something. Before I got saved, I tried to quit drinking and smoking dope many times, but I never could. It wasn't until I finally made Jesus Christ the Boss of my life that I was able to stop those addictions that had control over me.

I finally got to the point where I said, "I don't have the strength to quit by myself. God, I need Your help." That's when God came on the scene and delivered me.

I have learned the secret of being content in any and every situation, whether well fed or hungry, whether living in plenty or in want. I can do everything through him who gives me strength. — Philippians 4:12,13 NIV

God is no respecter of persons. If He did it for me, He will do it for you too.

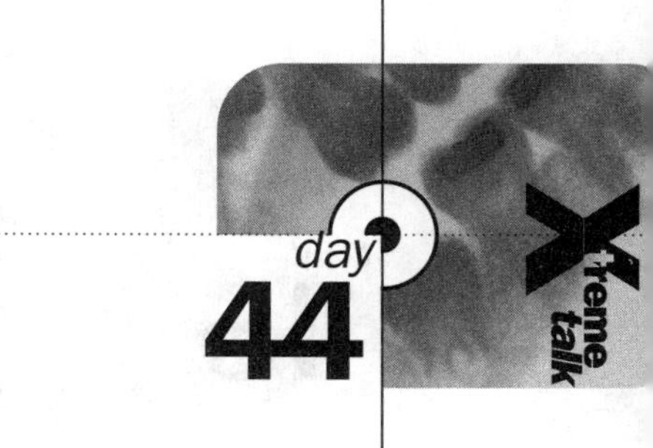

what is all this about a negative and positive confession?

The Bible tells us that our tongue has the power of life and death in it. It also says that we eat the fruit of what we say.

A lot of Christians believe that there is victory in knowing Jesus. But you would never guess it by the way some of them talk!

Check out your own confession. For instance, when was the last time you heard yourself say, "I will never be able to pass this test" or "Nobody likes me"? Well, with faith like that, you might as well hand the oars of your boat over to the devil right now!

Satan loves it when you start to doubt God's Word. He knows that when you do that, you are actually doubting God Himself.

***The tongue has the power of life and death, and those who love it will eat its fruit. — Proverbs 18:21* NIV**

Speaking God's Word in faith is more than just the power of positive thinking. It is eating the fruit of life straight from your own lips!

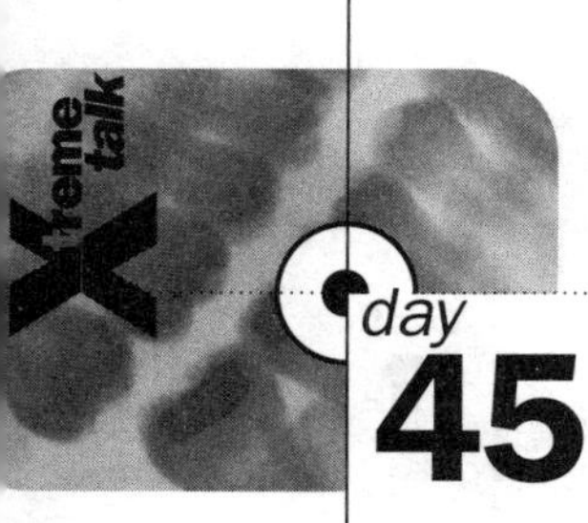

day
45

what does the Bible say about saving and spending money?

God isn't into waste. In fact, after Jesus fed the five thousand, He told His disciples to gather all the pieces that were left over so nothing would be wasted. Now, think about that. Even though God supernaturally supplied much more than was needed that day, Jesus wanted to make sure that every bit of it was put to good use!

Jesus said, "Bring them here." Then he had the people sit on the grass. He took the five loaves and two fish, lifted his face to heaven in prayer, blessed, broke, and gave the bread to the disciples. The disciples then gave the food to the congregation. They all ate their fill. They gathered twelve baskets of leftovers. About five thousand were fed.
— Matthew 14:18-21 THE MESSAGE

If you aren't faithful with the money God has already given you, how can you expect Him to give you more? So purpose in your heart not to be wasteful. Take care of and respect what you have. If God sees that you are faithful, He will just keep blessing you with more!

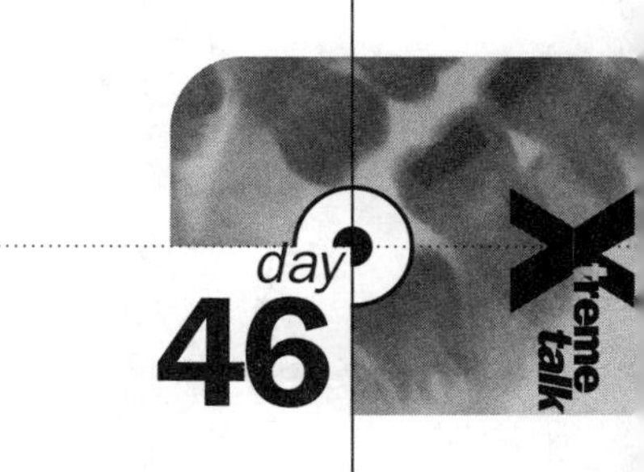

do I have to live like a Christian to go to heaven?

After we give our lives to God, He gives us the desire to become more like Him. We can't help but want to learn as much about Him as possible.

Your goal in life should always be to become more and more like Jesus. If it isn't, you may still get to heaven, but you will miss out on many of the blessings and rewards God has planned for you.

That's why the Bible says we are to **be imitators of God, therefore, as dearly loved children** (Ephesians 5:1 NIV). However, you can't imitate someone you don't know.

You get to know someone by hanging around him. And if you hang around God's Word and around His people, you are hanging around God.

This is just one reason why it is important to find a church home. Going to church is easy and can be fun. Everyone needs to be encouraged and taught the Word, and a good church helps meet these needs.

God knew what he was doing from the very beginning. He decided from the outset to shape the lives of those who love him along the same lines as the life of his Son. The Son stands first in the line of humanity he restored. We see the original and intended shape of our lives there in him. After God made that decision of what his children should be like, he followed it up by calling people by name. After he called them by name, he set them on a solid basis with himself. And then, after getting them established, he stayed with them to the end, gloriously completing what he had begun.
— Romans 8:29,30 THE MESSAGE

So make a habit of hanging around God and faithfully attending church. It will help you reach your goal of renewing your mind and growing to be more like Christ.

day **47**

aren't we as Christians supposed to hang out with each other?

Sure, you are supposed to fellowship with other Christian teens. But as I minister to teenagers all over the nation, I notice that one of the greatest problems youth groups face is *cliques.* It is sad, but most young people don't try to increase their circle of love, leaving those on the outside of the circle with the feeling that they don't belong.

Romans 15:7 says that we are to accept one another just as Christ accepted us. We are to become what I call "clique-busters."

So make people feel comfortable around you. When you see somebody you don't know come to the youth group — live on the edge. Walk up to them with a friendly smile and a warm handshake, and welcome them to the youth group. You may even want to invite them to sit with you.

You will be amazed at how contagious your friendliness will become. Your friends will see you accepting someone new, and they will start doing the same.

So reach out and welcome one another to God's glory. Jesus did it; now you do it! Jesus, staying true to God's purposes, reached out in a special way to the Jewish insiders so that the old ancestral promises would come true for them. As a result, the non-Jewish outsiders have been able to experience mercy and to show appreciation to God. Just think of all the Scriptures that will come true in what we do! — Romans 15:7-9 THE MESSAGE

Be a "clique-*buster,"* not a "clique-*builder"!*

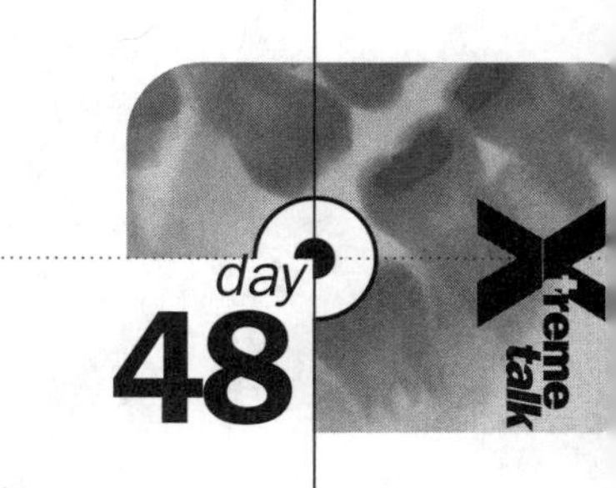

is it okay just to go to church, or do I need to get involved?

You develop spiritual strength and maturity when you stop just watching others do all the work of God's kingdom and start getting involved yourself. Hebrews 5:14 says that solid food is for the mature who by constant use have trained themselves to distinguish good from evil.

One night John Jacobs, the preaching power-lifter, and I were having dinner at his house. He showed me some of his baby pictures when he was just a few months old.

I thought to myself, *When I was two months old, I could have taken John on because I was bigger than he was!*

But what happened? John started pumping iron, building up his muscles, and today John's arms are bigger than both my legs put together! Why is he so much bigger than I am? Because he has exercised the muscles he has. As for me, I just like to ride my mountain bike.

But solid food is for the mature, who by constant use have trained themselves to distinguish good from evil. — Hebrews 5:14 NIV

So don't become a "spiritual doughboy." Be a participator, not a spectator, and watch your spirit man grow!

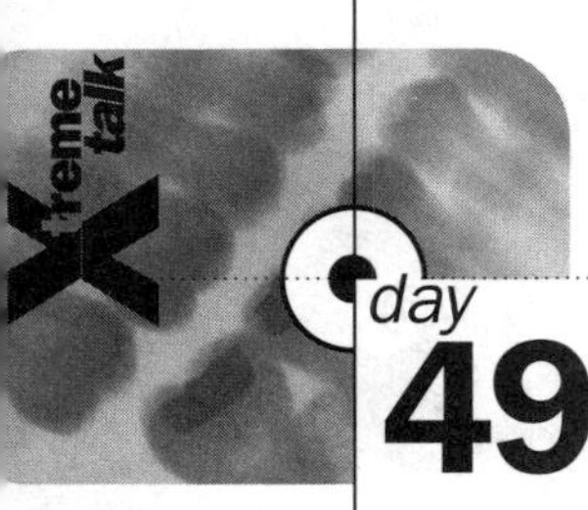

I am happy with the way my youth group is. why should I invite strangers?

In Acts 2:47, it says that each day the Lord added to the new group of believers others who were being saved.

Sometimes it is easy to forget that God has given you the responsibility for growth in your youth group and local church. That is why you need to be active in sharing your faith and getting others saved so that the kingdom of God can be built up.

Don't become satisfied and complacent with the way things are. If you do, you will end up cutting yourself short and possibly missing out on meeting someone whom God wants to use in a significant way in your life. As a matter of fact, He may even want to use you in a significant way in someone else's life.

Everyone around was in awe — all those wonders and signs done through the apostles! And all the believers lived in a wonderful harmony, holding everything in common. They sold whatever they owned and pooled their resources so that each person's need was met.

They followed a daily discipline of worship in the Temple followed by meals at home, every meal a celebration, exuberant and joyful, as they praised God. People in general liked what they saw. Every day their number grew as God added those who were saved. — Acts 2:43-47 THE MESSAGE

Don't limit God because you are satisfied. Assume the responsibility He has entrusted you with, and do what you can to help your youth group grow.

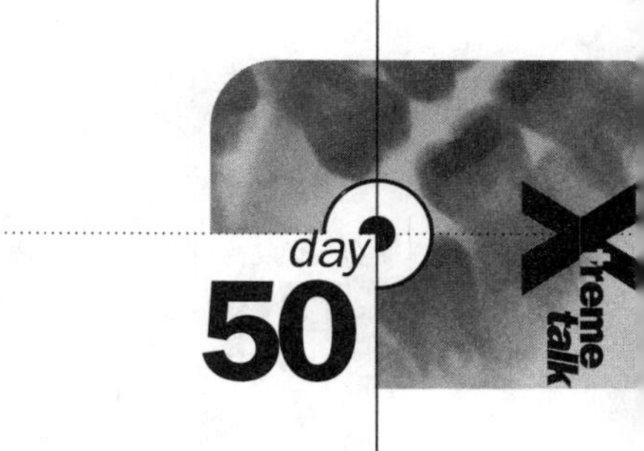

why should I inconvenience myself and invite others to church?

Why are you shying away from inviting your friends to church? Don't you want them to experience the joy you know in being a Christian?

If you really do want your friends, neighbors and family members to come to the Lord, you will have to use every means available to reach them. Inviting them to church is an easy way to expose them to the presence of God. Just think about it for a moment. An invitation to church can radically change a person's life forever.

Now, you might like to think it is the youth pastor's job to invite your friends from school to youth group. But the truth is, your friends are much more likely to come on your invitation than on the invitation of anybody else.

The fruit of the righteous is a tree of life, and he who wins souls is wise. — Proverbs 11:30 NIV

So take a moment to ask the Holy Spirit to bring to your mind some people He would like you to invite to your youth group or to church. Jot their names down on a piece of paper and determine to ask them to come with you. I dare you!

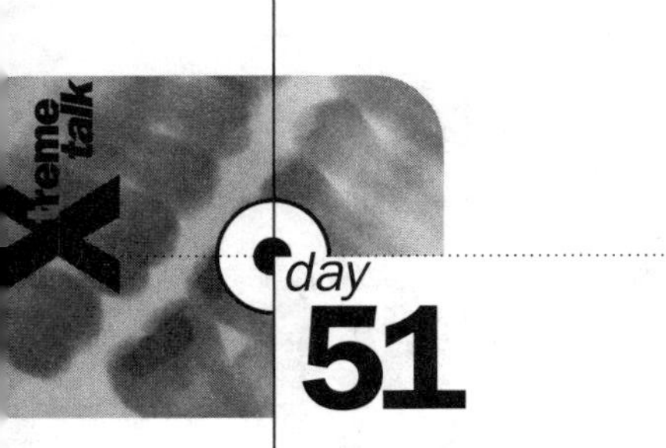

why does it feel bad to hear people swear?

The reason we feel that "lead ball" in our gut when we hear people using foul language is that our heart knows something that our mouth doesn't always live up to: First and foremost, the primary reason for communication is so we can fellowship with God.

When you hear others abuse their ability to communicate through cursing, name-calling or ripping somebody to shreds with harsh words, a siren goes off on the inside of you saying, "Warning! Warning! Danger!"

Now, if it hurts your spirit to hear someone else use foul language, imagine what it does to your spirit to hear *yourself* speak those words.

From the fruit of his mouth a man's stomach is filled; with the harvest from his lips he is satisfied. The tongue has the power of life and death, and those who love it will eat its fruit. — Proverbs 18:20,21 NIV

I can tell you this — when it comes to the words of your mouth, the Bible leaves no room for gray areas. You are either speaking words of life, or you are speaking words of death. There is no in between. So make a quality decision today to speak words that give life.

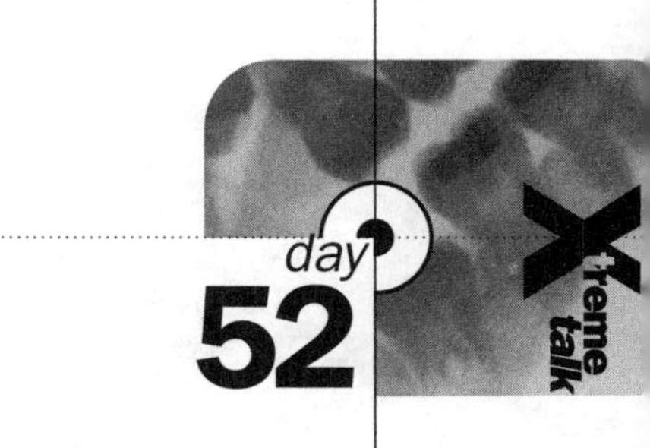

why shouldn't I listen to worldly music?

Music is powerful. It affects your thought life, and your thought life affects your spiritual life. Music is like food for your spirit.

God tells us in Romans 12:2 not to be conformed to the world but to be transformed by the renewing of our mind. When we listen to worldly music, our minds are being conformed to the world and its ways. On the other hand, when we listen to music written by God's people, it's easy to focus our mind on godly things. And who says that Christian music can't have a kick and a beat?

One of the great things about God is His creative nature. He created music both to praise Him and to teach us about Who He is. What a concept!

But even the devil knows how powerfully you can serve God when you use the gift of music He has created. So in order to keep you from praising God, the devil has perverted music to distract you.

***Do not conform any longer to the pattern of this world, but be transformed by the renewing of your mind. Then you will be able to test and approve what God's will is — his good, pleasing and perfect will. — Romans 12:2* NIV**

You are the one who will have to make a decision as to what kind of music and lyrics you are going to feed your spirit with. Will it be the music of the world — or music that glorifies God?

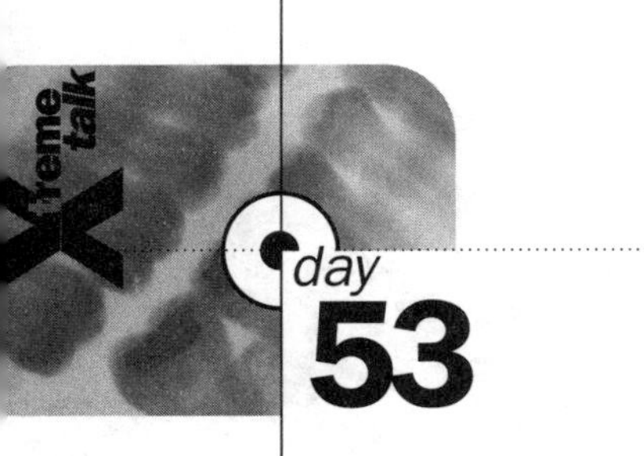

a lot of tv and movies have sexual content. should I stop watching them altogether?

The Bible says in Psalm 101:3 that we are to set before our eyes no vile thing.

It's true that TV and movies will pollute the way we think or act, especially when the programs and movies we watch are full of worldly junk. Why is that? Because God made us to receive natural information through our eyes and ears.

Now, of course, most of us wouldn't let strangers prance around our house in their underwear, nor would we invite someone over to our home so we could listen to him cuss us out for a while. And yet some television shows are just like that.

When we turn on the TV and watch that kind of ungodly garbage, we are really saying, "C'mon, cuss at me for a little while." We need to draw the line and refuse to watch that junk.

I will walk in my house with blameless heart. I will set before my eyes no vile thing. The deeds of faithless men I hate; they will not cling to me. Men of perverse heart shall be far from me; I will have nothing to do with evil. — Psalm 101:2-4 NIV

So choose your movies and television shows carefully. Remember, whatever you spend time seeing and hearing helps shape the person you are becoming.

how can I stop being moody?

Have you ever thought of moodiness as being a disguise for self-centeredness? Well, think about what First Corinthians 13 says. It is probably one of the most famous passages in the Bible, and it tells us what real love is.

Our attitude is like a huge neon sign that should always be flashing, "Jesus — Jesus — Jesus." But a lot of the time that invisible sign flashes, "Me — Selfishness — What Can I Get Out of This?"

I have been crucified with Christ and I no longer live, but Christ lives in me. The life I live in the body, I live by faith in the Son of God, who loved me and gave himself for me. — Galatians 2:20 NIV

So if you want to stop being moody, you have to decide that you are going to crucify your flesh. Get your focus off yourself, and become concerned with the needs of others as well.

is flirting okay?

Flirting is an issue that most people don't like to talk about because just about everyone has been guilty of doing it at one time or another.

But we don't need to get into a big philosophical discussion about why we flirt with the opposite sex, asking questions such as: Are we doing it innocently? Do we have false motives? Are we doing it just to be accepted?

One thing that concerns me more than flirting is that teenagers often become distracted and consumed with worry about what the opposite sex is thinking about them. When teenagers do that, they take their eyes off the goal of pleasing God and become entangled in pleasing others.

Do you see what this means — all these pioneers who blazed the way, all these veterans cheering us on? It means we'd better get on with it. Strip down, start running — and never quit! No extra spiritual fat, no parasitic sins. Keep your eyes on Jesus, who both began and finished this race we're in. Study how he did it. Because he never lost sight of where he was headed — that exhilarating finish in and with God — he could put up with anything along the way: cross, shame, whatever. And now he's **there,** ***in the place of honor, right alongside God. When you find yourselves flagging in your faith, go over that story again, item by item, that long litany of hostility he plowed through.*** **That** ***will shoot adrenaline into your souls! — Hebrews 12:1-3 THE MESSAGE***

Hebrews 12:1 tells us to throw off everything that hinders and the sin that so easily entangles us so we can run our spiritual race with our eyes fixed on Jesus. When we keep our eyes on the finish line rather than on what other people think about us, God will honor us for it.

is it possible to have my emotions healed after what I have been through?

Emotional healing can sometimes seem impossible. But remember, you have a promise that says with God, nothing is impossible. (Luke 1:37.)

One of the reasons why Jesus was anointed was to heal the brokenhearted. A lot of people think that God wants to slap them when they have a broken heart. But, no, He wants to *heal* their broken heart.

As one pastor said, when you become born again, you can turn your *scars* into *stars* — and that includes your emotional scars. Remember, you are a new creation. You may not feel like it all the time; in fact, it may take awhile before the reality hits you.

The Spirit of the Lord is on me, because he has anointed me to preach good news to the poor. He has sent me to proclaim freedom for the prisoners and recovery of sight for the blind, to release the oppressed, to proclaim the year of the Lord's favor. — Luke 4:18,19 NIV

But regardless of whether or not you feel like the new creation that God has made you, it is a fact. You are no longer bound to your past. God has a brand-new future for you. You will never be the same. He guarantees it!

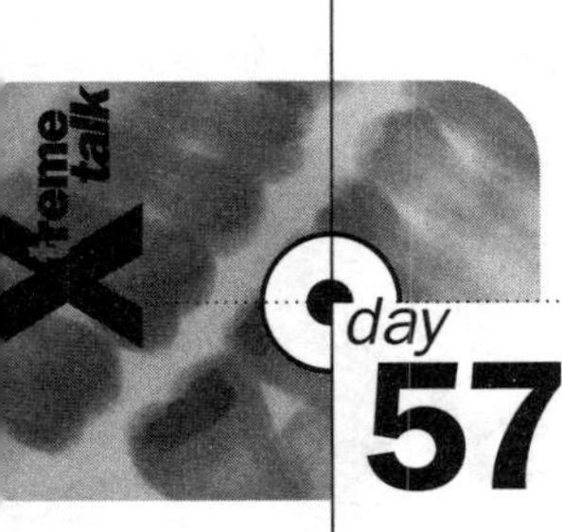

does God still heal through ministers, and why?

Yes, God does still heal, whether He does it through a minister or a friend or without anyone's help at all.

But even more importantly, we need to have this fact burned into our hearts and minds: God really does care about us. He wants us to be whole — spirit, soul *and* body.

The Bible says in Isaiah 53:5 that Jesus was wounded and crushed because of our sins. By taking our punishment, He has made us completely well. That is talking about bodily healing as well as spiritual healing.

Let me encourage you to believe for the best that God has for you. The complete and total healing of your body is a part of that best.

But he was pierced for our transgressions, he was crushed for our iniquities; the punishment that brought us peace was upon him, and by his wounds we are healed. — Isaiah 53:5 NIV

You can experience physical healing because, as a believer, you have been given power over all the works of the devil. So command every symptom of sickness to go, not only from your own body but from others' as well!

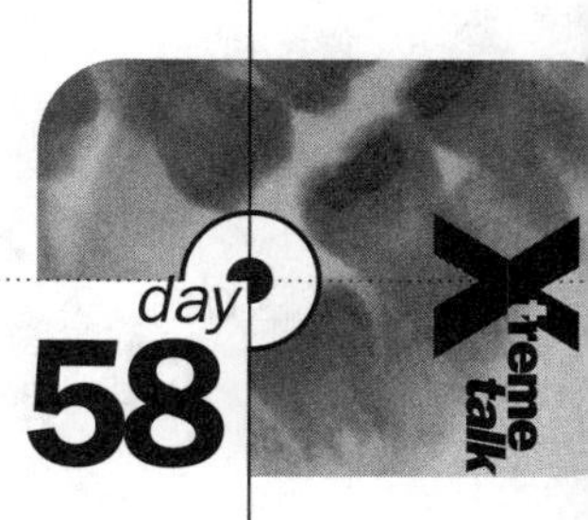

what is spiritual healing?

We have a promise in God's Word that says if we confess our sins, God is faithful and just to forgive us our sins and to cleanse us from all unrighteousness. (1 John 1:9.)

Spiritual healing is simply experiencing the forgiveness of God. It is something that happens instantly when we are born again.

When we decided to make Jesus Lord of our life, we gave Him permission to live inside of us through the Person of the Holy Spirit. Now we can stand before the presence of our heavenly Father just as though we never sinned.

When my little baby girl was born, no one looked at her and said, "Wow! She is the most beautiful bald-headed, no-toothed woman I have ever seen. It sure is a shame about her past." That would have been a pretty dumb thing to say because even though she didn't have any hair or teeth, she also didn't have any past.

It's the word of faith that welcomes God to go to work and set things right for us. This is the core of our preaching. Say the welcoming word to God — "Jesus is my Master" — embracing, body and soul, God's work of doing in us what he did in raising Jesus from the dead. That's it. You're not "doing" anything; you're simply calling out to God, trusting him to do it for you. That's salvation. With your whole being you embrace God setting things right, and then you say it, right out loud: "God has set everything right between him and me!" — Romans 10:8-10 THE MESSAGE

Well, when you get saved, neither do you. Your spirit has been made brand-new with no past; now you can begin again with a new start. That's what spiritual healing is all about!

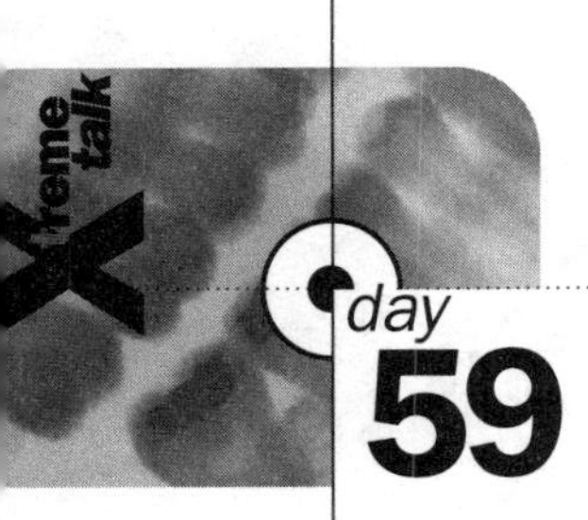

when will God not forgive me of my sins?

Matthew 6:14 says your heavenly Father will forgive you *if* you forgive those who sin against you.

Now, God is never going to ask you to do something He won't do Himself. The only reason you can forgive others is that He has already forgiven you. It makes it a whole lot easier to forgive when you realize that you have been forgiven.

I realized the truth of that fact just recently when I took my wife Angel on a date. After dinner, we were driving home, and a car pulled right out in front of me. I felt like yelling at that guy, "Hey, what are you doing?"

Then Angel calmly looked over at me, smiled and said, "It's a good thing you never did that to anybody before." Zingo, she got me! There is no telling how many times I have pulled out in front of other people!

In prayer there is a connection between what God does and what you do. You can't get forgiveness from God, for instance, without also forgiving others. If you refuse to do your part, you cut yourself off from God's part. — Matthew 6:14,15 THE MESSAGE

The next time you are tempted not to forgive somebody, just start thanking God for all the forgiveness you have received. It will be much easier then to let that unforgiveness go.

why is there all this attention drawn to someone who gets healed?

When God does something big in your life, it is really important to tell other people about it. It is that simple. You are just like a witness on the stand. You are testifying of the truth, the whole truth and nothing but the truth.

When someone asks you how you are doing, you could say, "Oh, fine," and no one would be very impressed. But when God has done something radical and explosive in your life, you should want to shout, "I am great! God has forgiven me of my sins!" or "He has healed my body!" or "He has filled me with His Spirit!"

Peter said, "I don't have a nickel to my name, but what I do have, I give you: In the name of Jesus Christ of Nazareth, walk!" He grabbed him by the right hand and pulled him up. In an instant his feet and ankles became firm. He jumped to his feet and walked.

The man went into the Temple with them, walking back and forth, dancing and praising God. Everybody there saw him walking around and praising God. They recognized him as the one who sat begging at the Temple's Gate Beautiful and rubbed their eyes, astonished, scarcely believing what they were seeing. — Acts 3:6-10 THE MESSAGE

When you testify, it brings out the truth so justice can be done. Therefore, whenever the Lord heals you or does something else special for you, be sure to tell others about it so God can receive the glory!

day
61

how difficult is it to have a good Christian relationship?

The Bible tells us, **As iron sharpens iron, so one man sharpens another** (Proverbs 27:17 NIV). Sharpening iron sure sounds like a lot of work, doesn't it?

A lot of people think this friendship stuff is supposed to be a piece of cake. Well, the truth is that every relationship in our life takes effort. You just don't throw away every friend in your life whenever things get bumpy.

So when the iron sparks start to fly between you and your friend, don't run for cover. Stick with that friend, and let God use that relationship to develop His kingdom.

As iron sharpens iron, so one man sharpens another. — Proverbs 27:17 NIV

You don't have to let the devil separate you from those who are sharpening your character. Let God do His perfect work in you as He continues to build you into the person He has called you to be!

what balance should you have between unsaved friends and Christian friends?

I believe one of the key elements to staying on fire for God is to hang around others who are on fire. Proverbs 12:26 tells you to choose your friends carefully because the way of the wicked will lead you astray.

Now, every one of us has a desire to feel accepted by our peers. And that isn't necessarily a bad thing, especially if we are hanging around "flame-throwers for Jesus." It can, however, be a bad thing if we are hanging around a bunch of "spiritual deadheads and lukewarmies" because even strong Christians can be influenced negatively by wrong friends.

A man of many companions may come to ruin, but there is a friend who sticks closer than a brother. — Proverbs 18:24 NIV

That is why the Word says that you are to choose your friends carefully. So think about the friends you currently have. Do you know where they stand in their relationship with God? Are your friends who aren't serving God snuffing out your flame? If so, you may need to reevaluate how much time you spend with them. It's much more important that you spend time with your "flame-thrower" friends who love Jesus.

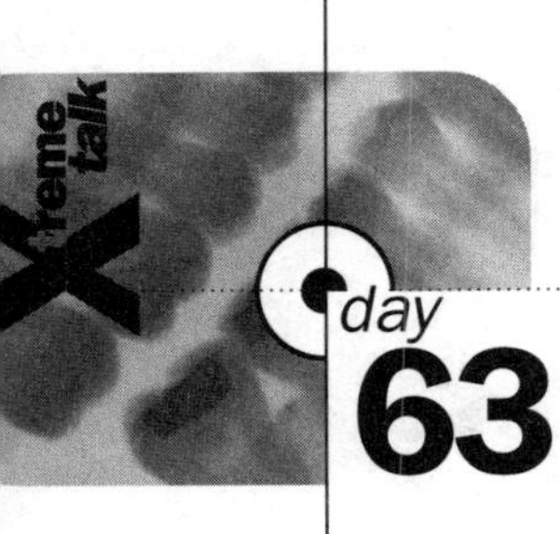

how should I let my non-Christian friends know that I'm a Christian?

If you are walking boldly with the Lord, you are like a fruit tree as you bear the fruit of the Spirit — love, joy, peace, patience, gentleness, goodness, faith, meekness and temperance. (Galatians 5:22-23.) When others see your fruit, they will know that you are different from those in the world. So don't keep your fruit to yourself. Give it away!

We Christians need to make sure that we don't always keep to ourselves, talking and fellowshiping only with each other one hundred percent of the time. No way! If that had been the way the Christians I knew had acted, I never would have been saved.

The fruit of the righteous is a tree of life, and he who wins souls is wise. — Proverbs 11:30 NIV

Sometimes you have to step out of your comfort zone and be a vessel of God's love to those who aren't saved yet. If you will do this, you will make a difference for God in this world.

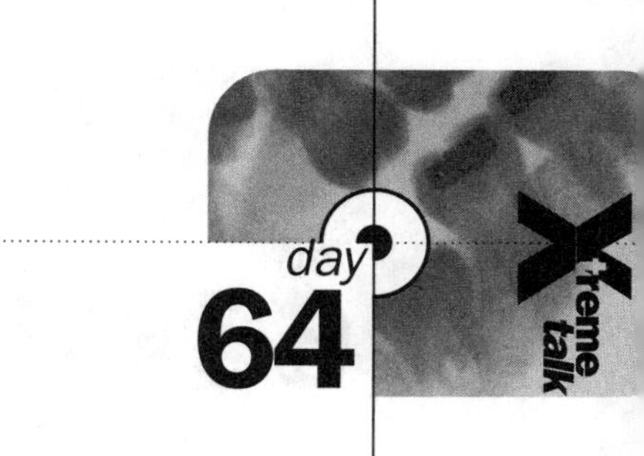

when bitterness and jealousy are the result of reaching out to people, why try anymore?

The Bible tells us in First Corinthians 3:3 that when there is jealousy and quarreling among us, it proves that we are worldly and not Christlike. Relationships can be such a delicate thing. In fact, success in a relationship really takes both parties being willing to contribute to the other person's character.

But it is impossible to contribute anything positive to others if you are envious or jealous about what they have or who they are. It is also very difficult to get your spirit quiet so you can hear from God when you are in constant strife with another person. You are too focused in on yourself and your bitterness.

You are still worldly. For since there is jealousy and quarreling among you, are you not worldly? Are you not acting like mere men? For when one says, "I follow Paul," and another, "I follow Apollos," are you not mere men? — 1 Corinthians 3:3,4 NIV

So go ahead — make a decision to live in unity with your brothers and sisters in Christ. If you do, your attitude won't be the thing that holds you back any longer. Instead, your decision to live in unity will propel you into new dimensions with the Lord!

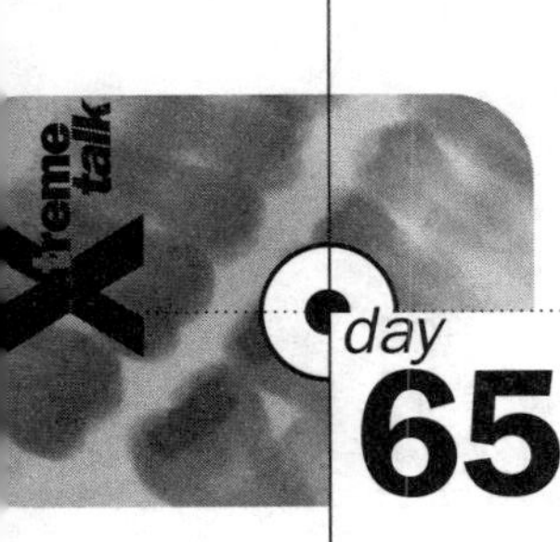

how far can I go with pride in myself and in my accomplishments?

Pride can come out in a lot of different ways. Sometimes you notice it when a person brags a lot. Sometimes you see it in people who can never admit they are wrong. Then there are those who try to impress all of the people all of the time.

Believe it or not, in most cases pride stems from insecurity. Our insecurity shows up in friendships when we don't really want to be vulnerable or honest in our communication with others because they might see our shortcomings.

Don't push your way to the front; don't sweet-talk your way to the top. Put yourself aside, and help others get ahead. Don't be obsessed with getting your own advantage. Forget yourselves long enough to lend a helping hand.

Think of yourselves the way Christ Jesus thought of himself. He had equal status with God but didn't think so much of himself that he had to cling to the advantages of that status no matter what. — Philippians 2:3-6 THE MESSAGE

It's fine to be proud of your accomplishments, as long as you realize that you were only able to succeed because God gave you the ability. But it's important to uproot every bit of the wrong kind of pride out of your life and put your security in God!

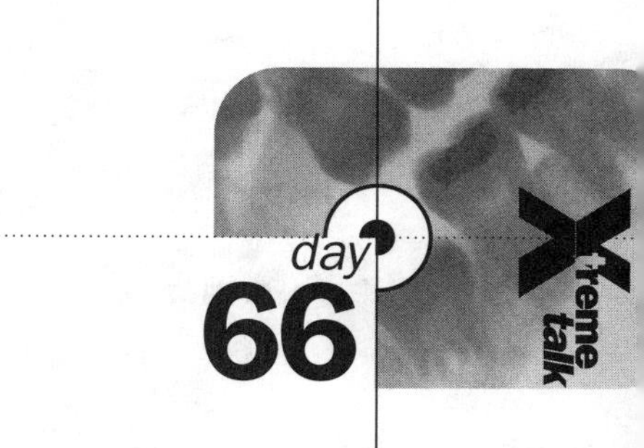

does wearing a Christian t-shirt put out a good message?

I love Christian t-shirts. One of the reasons they are so effective is that it is hard to backslide when you are wearing one. You have Jesus printed all over you!.

Another reason Christian t-shirts are effective is that you don't even have to open your mouth in order to preach a message wherever you go. Besides that, Christian t-shirts are a great way to start up conversations with others that might not otherwise occur.

Wearing clothes that proclaim Jesus is a great way to put Romans 1:16 in practice, which says that you are not ashamed of the gospel of Christ because it is the *power* of God to salvation to everyone who believes.

It's news I'm most proud to proclaim, this extraordinary Message of God's powerful plan to rescue everyone who trusts him, starting with Jews and then right on to everyone else! God's way of putting people right shows up in the acts of faith, confirming what Scripture has said all along: "The person in right standing before God by trusting him really lives."
— Romans 1:16,17 THE MESSAGE

So go ahead and put that Christian t-shirt on your chest, a smile on your face and the love of Jesus in your heart. When you do, you will make the devil so nervous, he will have to go out and buy himself a pair of Depends underwear!

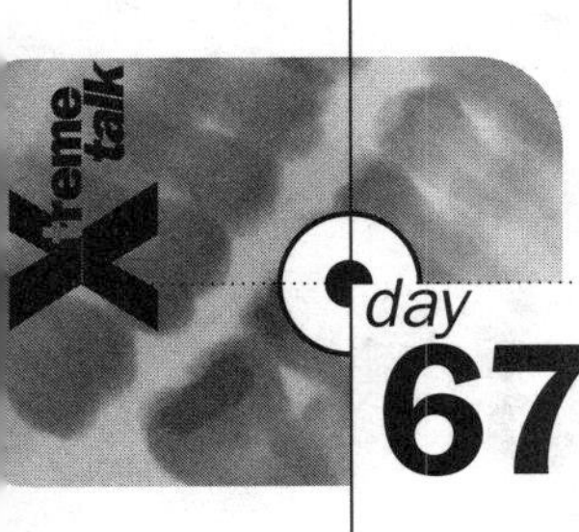

day
67

what good does it do to carry a Bible around with me?

It is the radical teenager who carries the Word of God with him to class. Some people say, "Carry your Bible to school? What for?" Listen, I know it sounds freaky, but that is exactly what we red-hot, boiling-over, flame-throwing Christians are — Jesus freaks!

The world has been trying to shove Christianity out of our schools for a long time. But they aren't going to succeed as long as young people are willing to bring the gospel back with them to school.

God means what he says. What he says goes. His powerful Word is sharp as a surgeon's scalpel, cutting through everything, whether doubt or defense, laying us open to listen and obey. Nothing and no one is impervious to God's Word. We can't get away from it — no matter what.
— Hebrews 4:12,13 THE MESSAGE

So go ahead — carry your Bible with you to school, and watch what God will do!

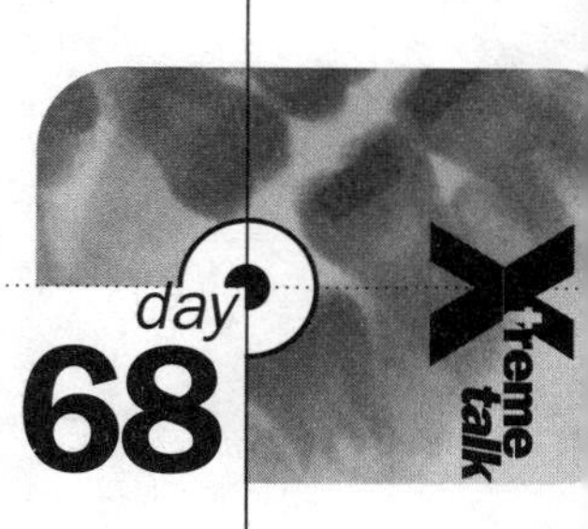

is it uncool to pray over my lunch at school?

Do you think someone isn't being cool just because they pray over their lunch in a public school? Are you kidding? Aren't we talking about cafeteria food here? The last time I saw that stuff, it needed *industrial-strength* prayer! But even if it doesn't need that strong of a prayer, it is ridiculous to believe that thanking God for your food is somehow going to make you uncool.

When you live for God, sometimes you have to take a chance and risk what others will think of you. You may have to take a bold step such as carry your Bible or pray over your lunch in order to make a difference.

***Do you think I speak this strongly in order to manipulate crowds? Or curry favor with God? Or get popular applause? If my goal was popularity, I wouldn't bother being Christ's slave. Know this — I am most emphatic here, friends — this great Message I delivered to you is not mere human optimism. I didn't receive it through the traditions, and I wasn't taught it in some school. I got it straight from God, received the Message directly from Jesus Christ. — Galatians 1:10-12* THE MESSAGE**

It is okay to be a positive form of peer pressure in your school. Yes, your peers are going to wonder more about you, but that's okay. Their wondering means they are going to ask questions. When they do, all you have to do is answer them. It's that easy. You can know where you stand and be bold about it.

what can I hope to accomplish by reading my Bible at lunch?

It is great to carry your Bible to school, but it is even more effective to take it out and read it. After all, didn't Jesus say in Matthew 4:4 that we couldn't live on bread alone? We need every word that God has spoken.

Your boldness will increase when you put your faith into action. The more you bring your Bible with you, the more courage will rise up in your heart, affecting other areas of your witness as well. Not only will you grow spiritually, but you will feel more confident in talking about your faith to your friends.

Jesus answered by quoting Deuteronomy: "It takes more than bread to stay alive. It takes a steady stream of words from God's mouth."
— Matthew 4:4 THE MESSAGE

And what do you do if some scoffer looks over as you are reading the Word and sarcastically asks, "Do you really believe that stuff?" You just look right back at him in surprise and say, "You don't?"

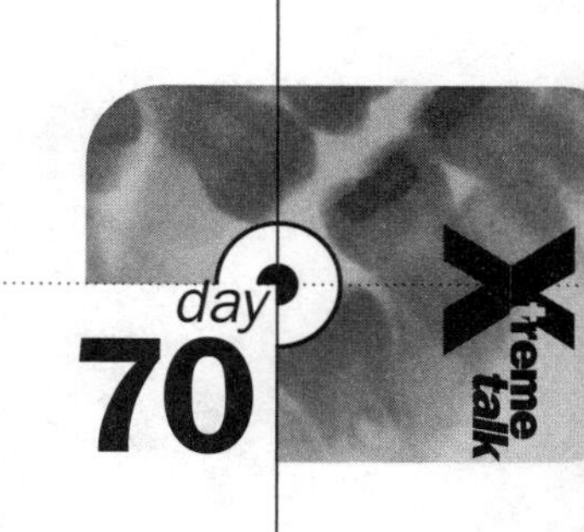

will reading my Bible in school give me an opportunity to witness?

The fact is, your school needs Jesus. I have a friend who told me something I have never forgotten. He said, "If we don't tell people the truth, somebody is going to tell them a lie."

When we do things that will cause us to stand up and be separate for the kingdom of God — such as wearing a Christian t-shirt, carrying a Bible, praying over our lunch or reading our Bible during study hall — people will notice that there is something different about us. Then they will begin to ask us questions. When that happens, all we have to do is answer their questions.

But in your hearts set apart Christ as Lord. Always be prepared to give an answer to everyone who asks you to give the reason for the hope that you have. But do this with gentleness and respect, keeping a clear conscience, so that those who speak maliciously against your good behavior in Christ may be ashamed of their slander. — 1 Peter 3:15,16 **NIV**

First Peter 3:15 says to always be prepared to give an answer to everyone who asks you the reason for the hope that you have. You are taking on the role of a witness in a court of law. And all a witness really does is just answer questions and tell the truth!

day

71

is being saved all that Jesus requires of me, or is there more?

Spiritual prosperity means, in part, that you are walking in the fullness of God's mercy. Proverbs 28:13 says that he who conceals his sins doesn't prosper, but the person who confesses and renounces them is the one who finds mercy.

When we are born again, the mercy of God is instantly available to meet our needs. But finding mercy should not be a one-time experience. Mercy is something we need to walk in daily.

The Lord has a ton of things He wants to do with our lives, but sometimes He is hindered by our own limited thinking. We think that just as long as we have met the requirement of being saved, everything else is extra credit.

When we think that way, we miss out on all of the good things God has planned for us here right now. We end up being satisfied with the continuance of sin in our lives, which puts God's plans for us on hold.

He who conceals his sins does not prosper, but whoever confesses and renounces them finds mercy. — Proverbs 28:13 NIV

All we have to do is ask God for His mercy to help us, and His mercy will be there to meet our need.

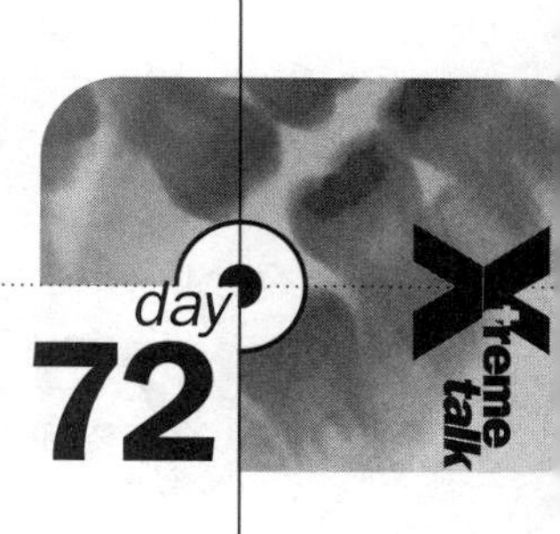

does favor have something to do with God's plan to prosper me?

How many times have we put God in a box by thinking that He only wants to meet our spiritual needs? And then there are those who think that He only wants to meet our physical needs.

But I have some good news. The Bible says that God gives us *all* things that pertain to life and godliness! (2 Peter 1:3.) That means He wants to meet all the needs of our lives, which would include our physical and our spiritual needs.

I remember when Angel and I first set out to travel as evangelists, we were believing God for a motor home. We didn't have a lot of money, but we did have faith that God would provide.

Then God granted me favor with a dealership owner. The car dealer didn't even want a tax write-off. I just handed him one-third of what he was asking, and he gave me the keys to a brand-new motor home.

Everything that goes into a life of pleasing God has been miraculously given to us by getting to know, personally and intimately, the One who invited us to God. The best invitation we ever received! We were also given absolutely terrific promises to pass on to you — your tickets to participation in the life of God after you turned your back on a world corrupted by lust.
— 2 Peter 1:3,4 THE MESSAGE

It doesn't matter who you are — God can give you favor to prosper you too. So make sure you don't put God in a box. Let Him prosper you in whatever way He sees fit.

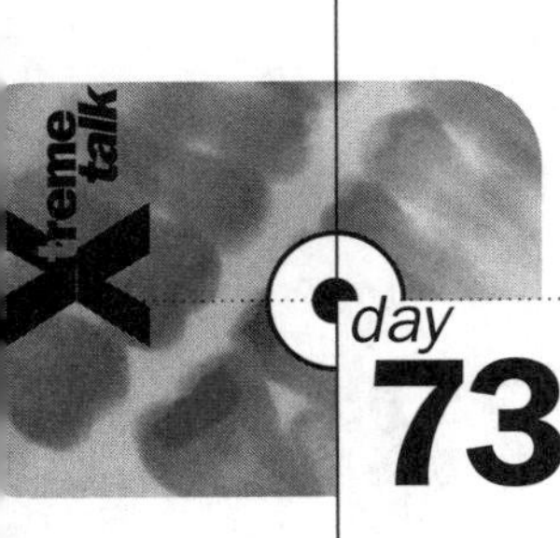

day
73

can I be sure God will heal me if I ask Him?

Part of God's plan to bless you includes healing and health. It is one thing to know that God is *able* to heal; it is another thing altogether to know that God is *willing* to heal.

Here's something that has helped me get a handle on God's willingness to heal: Only once in the entire Bible did anyone ever pray, "If thou wilt" concerning sickness and disease. That one instance, of course, was when the leper prayed, **If thou wilt, thou canst make me clean** (Matthew 8:2). Then the God of compassion answered that question once and for all by saying, *"I will."* When the leper heard that response, he stretched out his hand and was made whole.

Dear friend, I pray that you may enjoy good health and that all may go well with you, even as your soul is getting along well. — 3 John 2 NIV

Now I no longer question if it is God's will to heal me. I *know* that God is not only able to heal me, but He is willing as well.

if I tithe and am faithful to God, will He bless me even if I don't have much money?

The Bible tells us in Proverbs 3:9,10 that we are to honor the Lord with our wealth, which is the firstfruits of our crops. When we do that, our barns will be filled to overflowing and our containers will brim over with new wine.

When we honor God with our tithe, which is one-tenth of our income, we are worshipping Him as our Provider. It isn't so important *how much* we give as it is *the proportion* we give. Ten percent of all we earn belongs to Him, regardless of how big or small that ten percent is.

It isn't that God needs our money, because He owns the cattle on a thousand hills. (Psalm 50:10.) Rather, He requires us to tithe because He knows that where we put our money is an indication of what we value. And He wants our *heart* much more than He wants our *money.*

When we give the Lord our tithes and offerings, we are making a bold statement of faith, saying, "Lord, I give this tithe or this seed out of obedience, knowing that You are my Source of every good and perfect gift that comes my way. I'm depending on *Your* ability, not my own, to bring me through."

"Bring the whole tithe into the storehouse, that there may be food in my house. Test me in this," says the Lord Almighty, "and see if I will not throw open the floodgates of heaven and pour out so much blessing that you will not have room enough for it." — Malachi 3:10 NIV

Now take a look at how you have spent your money over the past week. If you have a checkbook, glance back over your spending for the past month and see where your money has gone. Are you honoring God with your money?

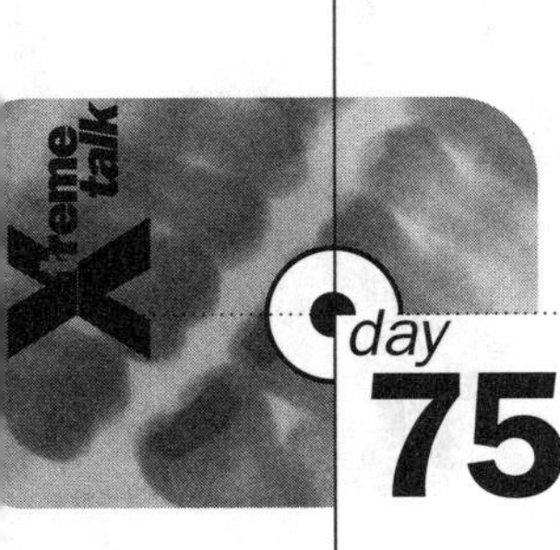

what does it mean to be emotionally prosperous?

Now, *that* is a good question!

God desires for us to have everything He has promised us, and that includes emotional stability. Hebrews 6:18 tells us that the hope God gives us is an anchor for the soul, firm and secure. Our soul is made up of our mind, will and emotions, and God has given us the hope to keep all three parts of our nature stable and secure.

That doesn't mean you won't have the opportunity to let your mind, will and emotions get out of control. But if you will renew your mind by reading and meditating on God's Word, I can promise you this: You will line up your thoughts with God's thoughts, and you will be able to get off your emotional roller coaster.

***When people make promises, they guarantee them by appeal to some authority above them so that if there is any question that they'll make good on the promise, the authority will back them up. When God wanted to guarantee his promises, he gave his word, a rock-solid guarantee — God can't break his word. And because his word cannot change, the promise is likewise unchangeable. — Hebrews 6:16-18* THE MESSAGE**

God wants you to be mentally and emotionally steady and strong. So get into God's Word, and allow Him to become an anchor for your soul.

can having an abortion affect my spiritual life?

Sometimes it's hard for me to believe that today's teenagers have to face something as politically potent as abortion. But the truth is, abortion is not just a political issue; it's a spiritual issue. Abortion is an issue that arises out of desperation, and no amount of politics can heal a desperate heart. Only Jesus can do that.

When you are in the middle of a dire situation, sometimes it is hard to really see that God does have a purpose for your life. His power is available to help you in any situation.

If you find yourself living in desperation and possibly contemplating an abortion, realize that God loves you. He isn't mad at you, and He wants you to come home to Him.

This day I call heaven and earth as witnesses against you that I have set before you life and death, blessings and curses. Now choose life, so that you and your children may live and that you may love the Lord your God, listen to his voice, and hold fast to him. For the Lord is your life, and he will give you many years in the land he swore to give to your fathers, Abraham, Isaac and Jacob. — Deuteronomy 30:19,20 NIV

Don't commit any act out of desperation. Give your life to God, and then just watch what He will do.

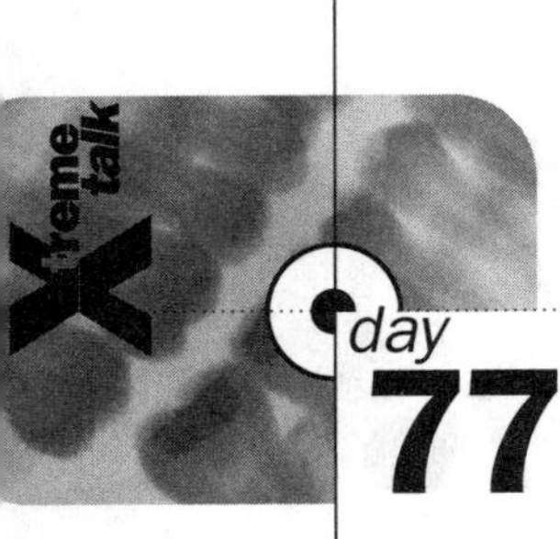

day

77

how do I know that God will stand with me if I don't join a gang?

Jesus makes a powerful statement in John 10:10 NIV: **The thief comes only to steal and kill and destroy.** But then Jesus goes on to say, **I have come that they may have life, and have it to the full.** I like that Scripture because the only thing that can truly keep you out of trouble and away from gangs and violence is your decision to follow Jesus Christ with your whole heart.

When you make that decision, you can count on God to be your Father. You won't need a substitute "family" that only leads you into death and destruction. Rely on your heavenly Father, and He will provide you with new friends. He will prosper you by giving you a more satisfying life.

Accept the life that He gives. It doesn't matter what the devil tries to do to destroy your youth; God is still able to raise up a generation that seeks Him fully. He is the One Who will give you a dream, a vision, a purpose and a reason to get out of bed in the morning.

A thief is only there to steal and kill and destroy. I came so they can have real and eternal life, more and better life than they ever dreamed of.
— John 10:10 THE MESSAGE

So make up your mind not to give in to peer pressure; instead, determine that *you* are going to be the peer pressure that draws others to Jesus.

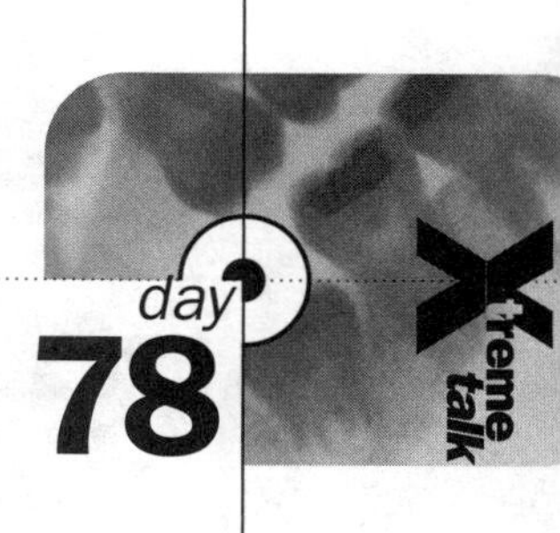

safe sex is an important issue, but when is it safe?

I once had a teenager tell me that the only thing that can truly protect you in sex is a wedding ring. In other words, the only kind of *safe* sex is *saved* sex.

God's Word says that our spirit, soul and body are to be kept strong and blameless until Christ comes back. (1 Thessalonians 5:23 NIV.) A wedding ring (and the lifetime commitment to one mate that it stands for) is the only thing that can protect all three parts of our being from danger.

You see, sex is more than just a physical act that involves your body. It involves your soul and spirit as well. And when you cross that line of intimacy with someone who isn't your husband or wife, you dangerously attach yourself to someone with whom you haven't made a godly covenant through marriage vows.

It is God's will that you should be sanctified: that you should avoid sexual immorality; that each of you should learn to control his own body in a way that is holy and honorable, not in passionate lust like the heathen, who do not know God; and that in this matter no one should wrong his brother or take advantage of him. The Lord will punish men for all such sins, as we have already told you and warned you. For God did not call us to be impure, but to live a holy life. Therefore, he who rejects this instruction does not reject man but God, who gives you his Holy Spirit. — 1 Thessalonians 4:3-8 NIV

Believe me, God's plan is the best plan. Stay sexually pure for marriage, because the safest sex of all is the sex you have saved for marriage. Remember, safe sex is *saved* sex.

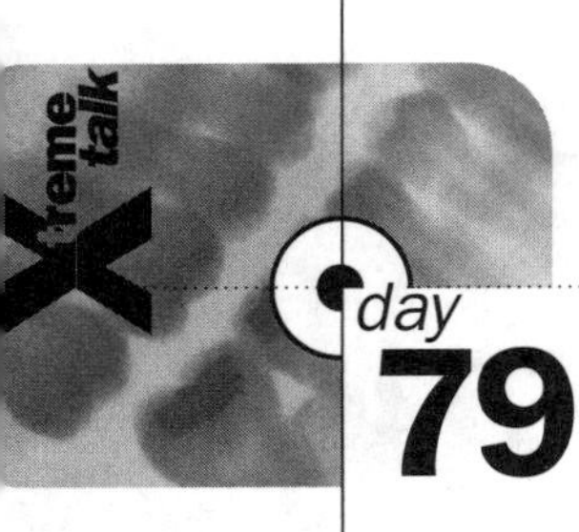

day
79

will Jesus bring me more satisfaction than drugs and alcohol?

Everybody is looking for a real experience. To someone who hasn't found Christ, drugs and alcohol can seem like a legitimate substitute. But look at what *The Living Bible* says in Romans 12:2: **Don't copy the behavior and customs of this world, but be new and a different person with a fresh newness in all you do and think. Then you will learn from your own experience how his ways will really satisfy you.**

I like that because God's ways do satisfy us. His ways are the only ways that won't leave us empty.

***Do not conform any longer to the pattern of this world, but be transformed by the renewing of your mind. Then you will be able to test and approve what God's will is — his good, pleasing and perfect will.* — *Romans 12:2* NIV**

With all that is happening around us, it is time for the church to wake up and start giving teenagers the *real* experience of true salvation that only comes through Jesus. Jesus, and *only* Jesus, can transform this generation and this world.

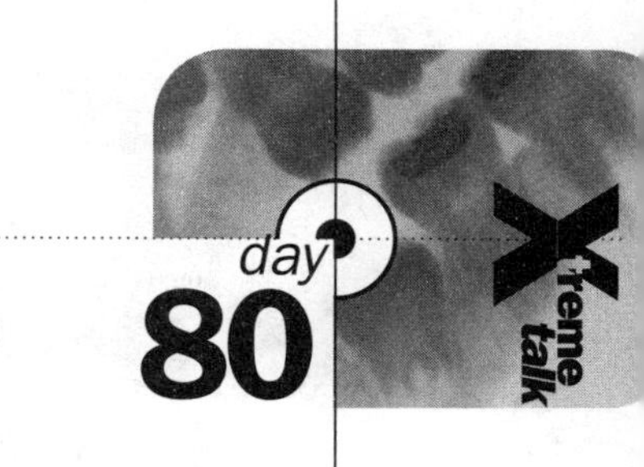

our generation seems hopeless; will it be able to stand up for Jesus Christ?

Every discussion about Generation X ultimately boils down to each person's expectations of the youth of this world. The problem is that most people believe this generation of youth lacks expectations of *themselves.* Young people are perceived as lacking hope.

But I don't think that is necessarily true. I travel all over this nation speaking to teenagers in every walk of life, and I see thousands of them come to Christ every single year. They are putting hope back in their lives and are making eternal decisions for God.

"In the Last Days," God says, "I will pour out my Spirit on every kind of people: Your sons will prophesy, also your daughters; your young men will see visions, your old men dream dreams." — Acts 2:17 THE MESSAGE

Thousands of young people in this generation are seeking God and putting the standards of Christ back into America. This isn't Generation X — it's a generation of expectancy!

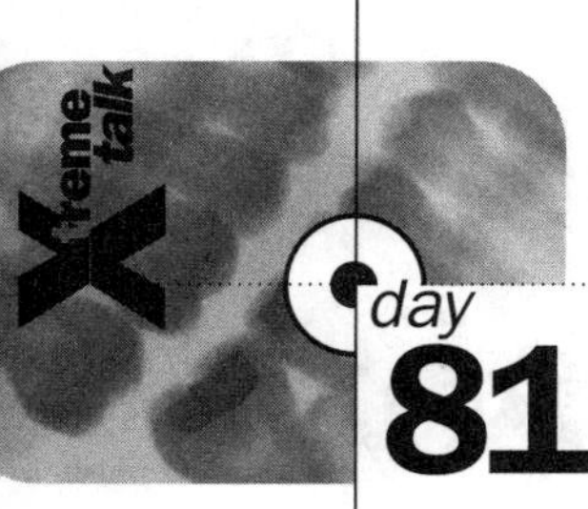

why is it that I find Christians who cheat?

Unfortunately, not everybody who says he is a Christian always acts like one. His relationship and trust in God may be seriously lacking.

Think about it for a moment: How would it look for you to tell your friends, "My God will supply all of my needs" and then to turn around and cheat on a test or an assignment? Do you realize what you essentially would be saying? "Just in case God doesn't pull through, I'd better handle this one myself." In that situation, your trust is more in yourself than it is in God.

Now, you can know this for sure: Cheating is wrong! I know that most people don't set out to cheat or cut corners. But in the middle of a high-pressure situation when it looks as though no one will find out what a person has done, it could be easy for that person to compromise.

There is one test we will never be able to cheat on — the test of our character and our integrity. It is the ultimate pop quiz. The only way we can pass this test is to act on what we think Jesus would do in a given situation.

This is the confidence we have in approaching God: that if we ask anything according to his will, he hears us. And if we know that he hears us — whatever we ask — we know that we have what we asked of him.
— 1 John 5:14,15 NIV

When our friends see that our integrity is something we act on instead of something we just talk about, they will know we are serious about serving the Lord.

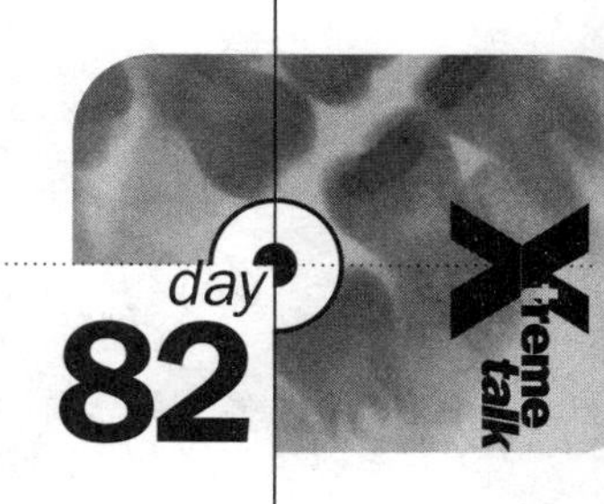

why should I respect adults when so many lie and openly live together unmarried?

Did you ever stop to wonder why a lot of people think it is cool or funny when you act disrespectfully toward the adults in your life? I don't pretend to know what goes on in the mind of every teenager, but I can remember being one. And I wondered even back then why some teens think it's cool to show disrepect.

God brings certain adults across young people's path to help and instruct them. However, many teenagers tend to think that all the adult influences in their lives are wrong. These teens have developed a disrespectful attitude toward all adults.

As Christians, we don't have any excuse for being disrespectful. Jesus should be our ultimate Teacher and Role Model, and He is never wrong. To show disrespect to an adult is to veer from the instruction of the Lord. That is neither funny nor cool. It is just dumb.

***Rise in the presence of the aged, show respect for the elderly and revere your God. I am the Lord. — Leviticus 19:32* NIV**

Even though some of the adults you know may not set the kind of example you should follow, take the initiative and become an example worthy of being followed by your peers, teachers, parents and all the other adults in your life. Remember, you aren't responsible to God for their actions; however, you *are* responsible for *your* actions, so make them count for the good.

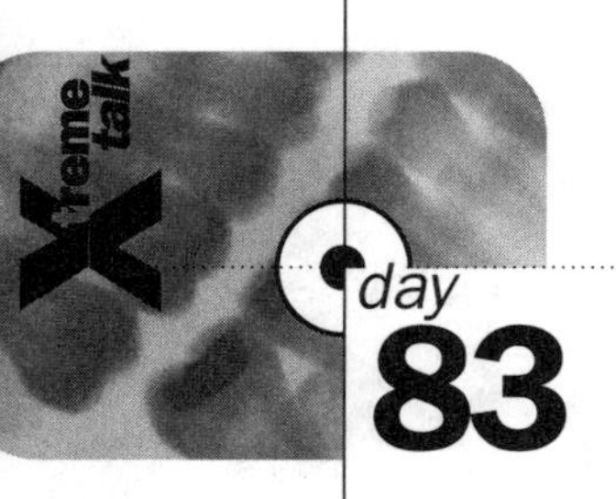

why is a good attitude important?

There are always opportunities for us to lose a joyful attitude because of all the circumstances that come our way. But we need to realize that attitude is contagious. The Bible tells us that we are to have the same attitude as Christ. (Philippians 2:5 NIV.)

Don't make any mistake about it; our attitude is *our* responsibility and nobody else's. People notice when our attitude goes bad even once. They also notice if we stay full of joy. When the joy of the Lord is our strength, people will want to have what we have.

But that's no life for you. You learned Christ! My assumption is that you have paid careful attention to him, been well instructed in the truth precisely as we have it in Jesus. Since, then, we do not have the excuse of ignorance, everything — and I do mean everything — connected with that old way of life has to go. It's rotten through and through. Get rid of it! And then take on an entirely new way of life — a God-fashioned life, a life renewed from the inside and working itself into your conduct as God accurately reproduces his character in you. — Ephesians 4:20-24 THE MESSAGE

So draw on the joy of the Lord as your strength, and hang on to a good attitude — no matter *what* comes your way!

why is it important not to lie?

The book of Proverbs has a lot to say about our words. The words of our mouth are actually extensions of ourselves.

Most of us know that lying is wrong because of the "thou shalt not" list in the Ten Commandments. (Exodus 20:16.) But *why* is lying wrong?

I think the primary reason it's wrong is that it hurts other people as well as yourself. Even little white lies and half-truths can be just as destructive as full-fledged lies.

Since lying is learned behavior, it can be unlearned, but it will take a real desire on your part to come clean. It can be done, and the habit of lying can be broken. Just think of how free you could be by just telling the truth. You wouldn't have to keep track of your lies anymore!

To the Jews who had believed him, Jesus said, "If you hold to my teaching, you are really my disciples. Then you will know the truth, and the truth will set you free." — John 8:31,32 NIV

Jesus said that you will know the truth, and the truth will set you free. (John 8:32.) So don't close yourself off from the blessings of God. Stop lying!

day

85

why not skip a few classes when there's something better going on?

You just want to miss a few classes. Nobody is going to notice, right? Wrong. Someone *will* notice. First John 3:20 tells us that God knows everything.

Ditching class can be a huge temptation, and sometimes it can seem very easy to justify. But we need to get to the bottom line. When we don't do something (such as go to class) that we know we are supposed to do, we are either being lazy or disobedient or both.

I don't know about you, but I have a very hard time justifying either laziness or disobedience in the light of God's Word. Our education is important. It is something we can't take for granted.

***Dear children, let us not love with words or tongue but with actions and in truth. This then is how we know that we belong to the truth, and how we set our hearts at rest in his presence whenever our hearts condemn us. For God is greater than our hearts, and he knows everything. — 1 John 3:18-20* NIV**

God rewards diligence. Don't skip out on a chance to change lives, namely your own. If you are ditching, you are missing.

what's the matter with playing a little joke on someone every now and then?

Proverbs 26:18,19 tells us that anyone who deceives his neighbor and says, "I was only joking," is like a madman who shoots arrows. That puts a clearer perspective on the way we joke with people, doesn't it?

Sometimes we forget how powerful our words can be. It may not seem like a big deal to us when we kid around with somebody in a cruel way, but more than likely, it is a very big deal to them.

Aren't we supposed to love our neighbor like ourselves? If we really believe this, we are going to take into account how other people feel.

***Like a madman shooting firebrands or deadly arrows is a man who deceives his neighbor and says, "I was only joking!" – Proverbs 26:18,19* NIV**

It is time to exercise self-control over your tongue. Don't make cruel comments about others. It doesn't matter if you are joking. If you shoot deadly arrows, those arrows will one day come shooting back at you.

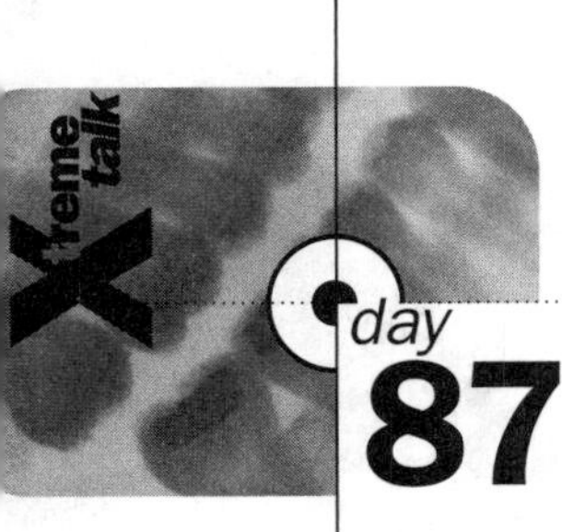

why be nice to people who continue to be mean to you?

Sometimes it can be easy to get offended by other people and just want to "flesh out." Haven't you heard that saying, "Don't get mad, get even"?

But Jesus has a higher standard than that for dealing with others. In fact, His message is one of total humility. He says in Luke 6:29 NIV, **If someone strikes you on one cheek, turn to him the other also.**

So *having* the love of Christ means that you *act on* it as well. It is easy to love the loveable people in your life, but it takes a real man or woman to put aside offenses and love those who aren't very loveable.

To you who are ready for the truth, I say this: Love your enemies. Let them bring out the best in you, not the worst. When someone gives you a hard time, respond with the energies of prayer for that person. If someone slaps you in the face, stand there and take it. If someone grabs your shirt, giftwrap your best coat and make a present of it. If someone takes unfair advantage of you, use the occasion to practice the servant life. No more tit-for-tat stuff. Live generously. — Luke 6:27-31 **THE MESSAGE**

That's the kind of integrity that is going to give you a big reward. All you have to do is take in a deep breath and then slowly let it go. Don't flesh out.

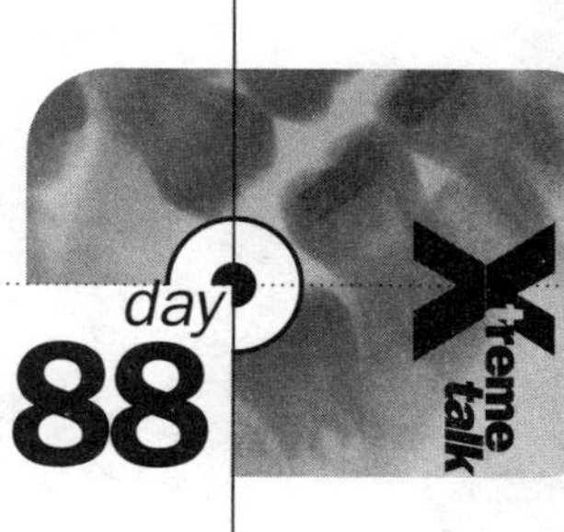

why reach out to unpopular people when they will just drag you down?

We all know somebody who is viewed at school as unpopular, ugly or even an outcast. It is easy to stay busy witnessing to our friends in our own circles, pretending that these other people just aren't there. But the truth is, the person at our school who is looked down on by others needs Jesus just as badly as the folks we call our friends.

Don't be worried about what your friends will think if they see you associating with someone who is considered an outcast. Who knows — they may even respect you more for it because you were braver than they were!

Besides, you are in good company because Jesus also associated with outcasts. He believed that loving His neighbor meant sharing His love with people regardless of the popularity He may or may not have gained from the action.

But he wanted to justify himself, so he asked Jesus, "And who is my neighbor?" "Which of these three do you think was a neighbor to the man who fell into the hands of robbers?" The expert in the law replied, "The one who had mercy on him." — Luke 10:29,36,37 NIV

So go ahead, take a chance. Give Jesus to somebody who isn't classified as "popular" or "cool," and extend your circle of love.

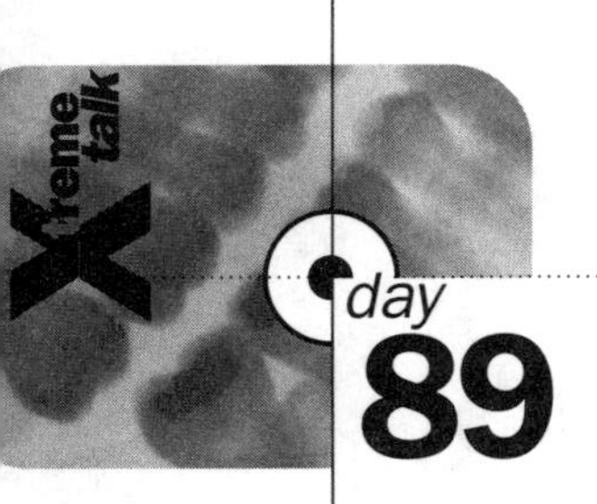

what does it accomplish to give to people?

Second Corinthians 9:8 talks about having all our needs met so we can abound to every good work. That tells me that God wants us to have more than enough so we can be a blessing to others. God doesn't care how old or young we are; He wants us all to practice the art of giving.

You may be thinking, *Yeah, but my friends don't appreciate the things I give to them.* Jesus told us that we need to lend to our enemies and not to expect anything back. If it works for our enemies, certainly it should work for our friends.

God can pour on the blessings in astonishing ways so that you're ready for anything and everything, more than just ready to do what needs to be done. As one psalmist puts it, "He throws caution to the winds, giving to the needy in reckless abandon. His right-living, right-giving ways never run out, never wear out." — 2 Corinthians 9:8,9 THE MESSAGE

Be generous with your things. Don't show them off, but let them be a blessing to others. As you do that, the Bible says that people will see your good works and glorify our Father which is in heaven. (Matthew 5:16.)

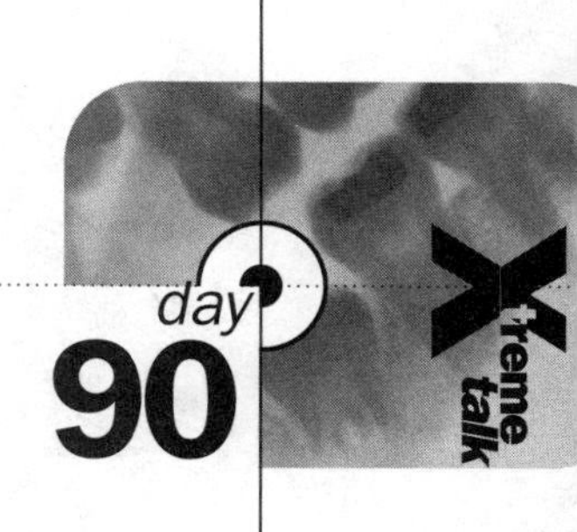

how can I be an encouragement to my friends at school?

When your friends get upset about something, you should be the first person they want to turn to for encouragement. Notice, I didn't say you should show them *sympathy.* Don't stoop to the devil's level by embracing the negative feelings of others. This may cause your friends to feel better for a while, but it won't really give them a hope they can hold on to.

Don't get me wrong. It's important to listen to people's problems and give them an opportunity to express how they feel about their situation. When you do that, you are showing *empathy.*

***He who answers before listening — that is his folly and his shame.* — *Proverbs 18:13* NIV**

But when it comes time for you to speak, let your friends know what *God* thinks about the situation. Sometimes you may even have to dig into the Word in order to find out God's perspective in the matter. But go ahead and take the time to do that. Then you can be an encouragement to your friends, giving them hope as you let them know of the future victory that is theirs through Jesus.

how can I take a bold stand for Jesus?

There are many important ways you can be a witness to others. For example, you can read your Bible at school, wear a Christian t-shirt, listen to Christian music and be sweet and kind to people.

But your Christian walk needs to be more than *visual;* it also needs to be *verbal.* You need to be bold enough to speak out about your belief in Jesus.

What would you do if you knew the Holy Spirit wanted you to share the gospel with one of your friends who was going to die soon? You wouldn't just wear a Christian t-shirt and hope that he would ask you a question so you could hand him a tract. No! Of course, you wouldn't.

You would bring up your relationship with Jesus in a conversation and tell him all about it. Then you would give him an opportunity to make a decision for himself.

The wicked man flees though no one pursues, but the righteous are as bold as a lion. — Proverbs 28:1 NIV

Since you never know when that day will come for the people you know, you need to pay attention to the leading of God's Spirit. He knows more than you do. If He prompts you to share with someone, just take a bold step and do it.

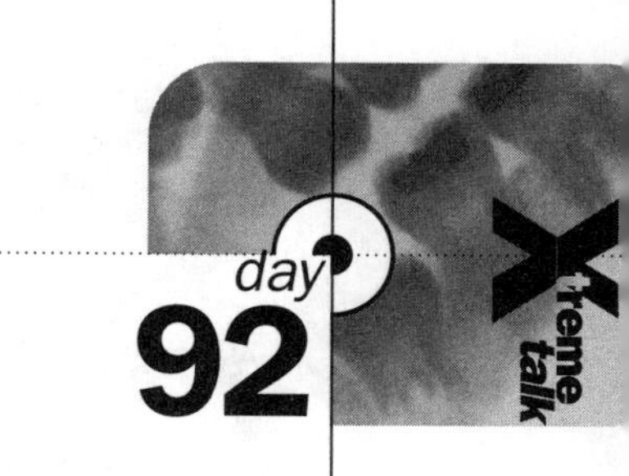

how can I effectively witness to others?

God's Word tells you that you need to *clothe* yourself with compassion. How does that work? Well, just think of it this way: The clothes you wear say something about who you are and how you feel.

For example, if you are a "laid back" sort of person, you probably wear more casual clothes. If you are cold all the time, more than likely you wear your clothes in layers. Your clothes communicate who you are.

***Summing up: Be agreeable, be sympathetic, be loving, be compassionate, be humble. That goes for all of you, no exceptions. No retaliation. No sharp-tongued sarcasm. Instead, bless — that's your job, to bless. You'll be a blessing and also get a blessing. — 1 Peter 3:8,9* THE MESSAGE**

In the same way, your compassion for others needs to be worn on the outside of your character. It isn't enough just to silently empathize in your mind. True compassion is an *action*. If you really want to make a difference for God with your friends, you are going to have to clothe yourself with compassion.

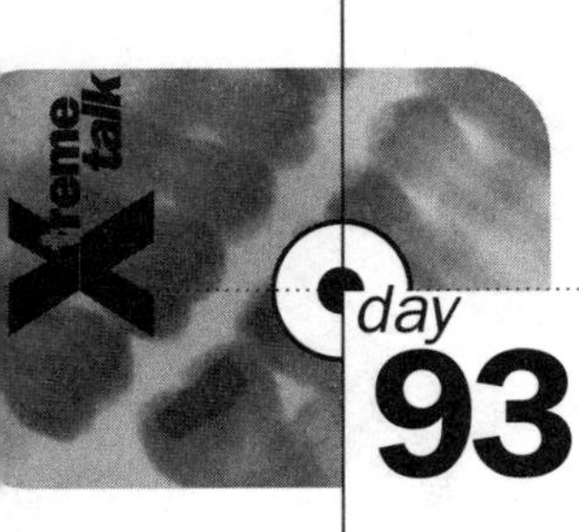

day
93

why do I always feel condemnation, like I'm not doing what I should be doing?

First of all, examine your heart and see if there may be sin in your life that the Holy Spirit is convicting you of or something He wants you to do. If you can't find anything, you are possibly carrying around a false sense of guilt and condemnation that the blood of Jesus has already taken care of.

So many Christians never get ahold of the truth in Romans 8:1, which says, **There is therefore now no condemnation to them which are in Christ Jesus.** The key phrase here is **them which are *in* Christ Jesus.**

You see, when you get saved, you are freed from condemnation. God isn't holding anything against you, and neither should you.

As far as others are concerned, you need to stop spewing condemnation on them as well. If they are Christians already, the Holy Spirit will convict them of their sins. He doesn't need you to do His work for Him.

And if they haven't received Jesus as their personal Lord and Savior, the Word says that they have been condemned already. Heaping even more condemnation on them isn't going to do any good.

Therefore, there is now no condemnation for those who are in Christ Jesus, because through Christ Jesus the law of the Spirit of life set me free from the law of sin and death. — Romans 8:1,2 NIV

As a matter of fact, the Bible tells us that it is the goodness of God that leads men to repentance. (Romans 2:4.) It is the heavenly Father's love and goodness that brings people back to Him. The Word is true, and love never fails.

why is it important to follow through with actions in my walk with Christ?

One thing the world hates about Christianity is the hypocrisy they have seen associated with the church throughout the years. Unfortunately, they have ample evidence to support their case.

We don't need to be concerned with what others have done by not living like Christ. But we do have to be concerned with the way our own lives represent Jesus to others.

If Christians would spend less time focusing on each other and more time focusing on their own integrity in their personal walk, we would have less problems.

Another key to being an effective witness is consistency. If we are out partying Saturday night with the same people we are inviting to church the next morning, what does that say about our commitment?

But the wisdom that comes from heaven is first of all pure; then peace-loving, considerate, submissive, full of mercy and good fruit, impartial and sincere. — James 3:17 NIV

The people who pressure us to compromise are the same people who will use compromise as a reason to reject the gospel. That's why consistency is so important.

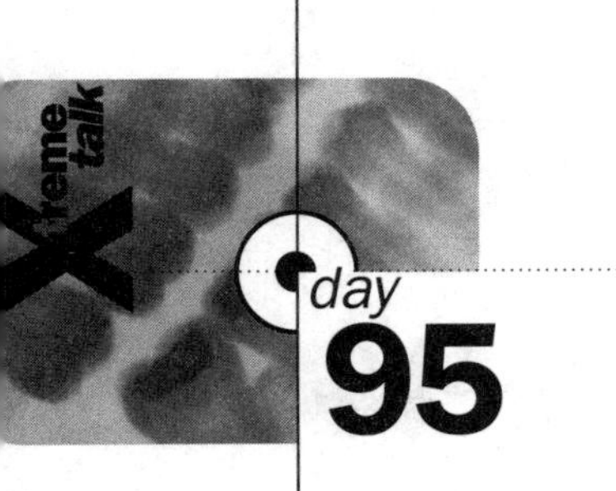

how can I be led by the Holy Spirit in witnessing to my friends?

Sometimes we get overly concerned about sharing Jesus with our friends because we think we are under some heavy obligation to preach to every kid who moves. We do have a responsibility to share God's good news with people, but it should never be out of a sense of drudgery or obligation.

Do you know that you can be led by the Spirit of God to witness to certain people at certain times? It is a much more effective way to witness because you know that what you are saying and doing is being directed by Him. And whether or not the person responds, you know that you have done your part at that time.

So your responsibility in sharing Jesus with your friends lies first in making sure that your spirit is in tune with the Spirit of God. How do you do that? By spending time talking to Him and being sensitive to His promptings throughout the day.

Second Timothy 1:6 calls that process "stirring up the gift of God that is in you." The gift, of course, is the Holy Spirit, and it is your responsibility to stir Him up in you. It isn't your pastor's, your parents' or your friend's responsibility. It is yours.

Therefore, brothers, we have an obligation — but it is not to the sinful nature, to live according to it. For if you live according to the sinful nature, you will die; but if by the Spirit you put to death the misdeeds of the body, you will live, because those who are led by the Spirit of God are sons of God. — Romans 8:12-14 NIV

So go ahead. Stir up the gift of God in you, and see what happens when you talk to others about the Lord!

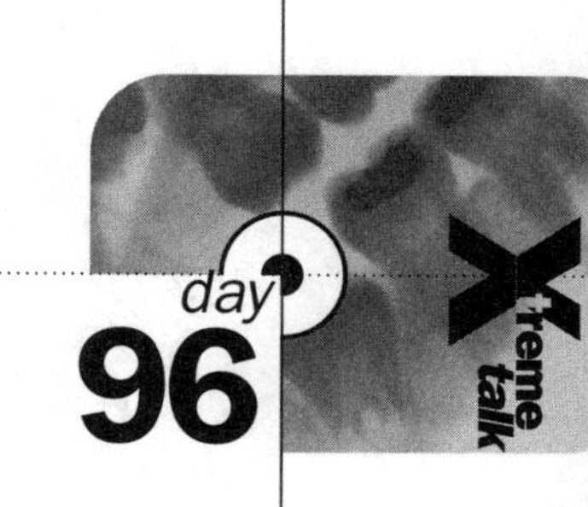

I am friendly to everyone, but not everyone smiles back. what should I do?

Relationships are important to God. The Bible tells us that if we walk in the light as He is in the light, we will have fellowship with one another. Ideally, God created this world to be free from conflict altogether, but that changed when sin entered into the world.

The reality is that we have plenty of opportunities to get rubbed the wrong way every day of our lives. Resolving conflict is just a part of daily living. The question is not *if* we will have conflict, because it will most certainly come. The real question is this: What will we do when conflict comes? Will we respond in love, or will we flesh out?

If we claim to have fellowship with him yet walk in the darkness, we lie and do not live by the truth. But if we walk in the light, as he is in the light, we have fellowship with one another, and the blood of Jesus, his Son, purifies us from all sin. — 1 John 1:6,7 NIV

To think that we will gel with everybody one hundred percent of the time is unrealistic thinking on our part, because we won't. However, if we will consciously act more and more on the Word of God and in His love toward others, we will see our relationships strengthened day by day.

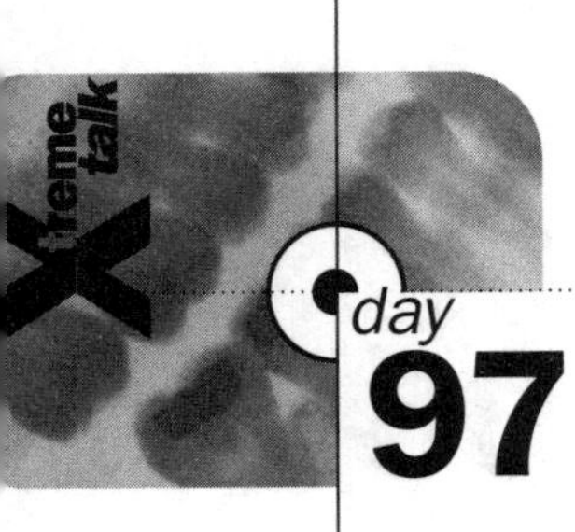

day
97

why is it important to be a loyal friend?

Are you the kind of person whom others can always count on?

One of the most frustrating things in the world is to have a friend who is constantly unreliable, late or who just doesn't do what he says he will do. If *you* are that kind of person, you need to look at what Proverbs says about keeping your word. Being a man or woman of your word is vital to your friendships and relationships with others.

For instance, Proverbs 11:3 NIV says that **the unfaithful are destroyed by their duplicity.** What in the world is *duplicity?* It is saying one thing and doing another. When you commit to something, you need to keep your word. After all, you are known by your actions.

The integrity of the upright guides them, but the unfaithful are destroyed by their duplicity. — Proverbs 11:3 NIV

Loyalty is more than just a nice quality to have; it is a necessity. So be faithful and keep your word, no matter what.

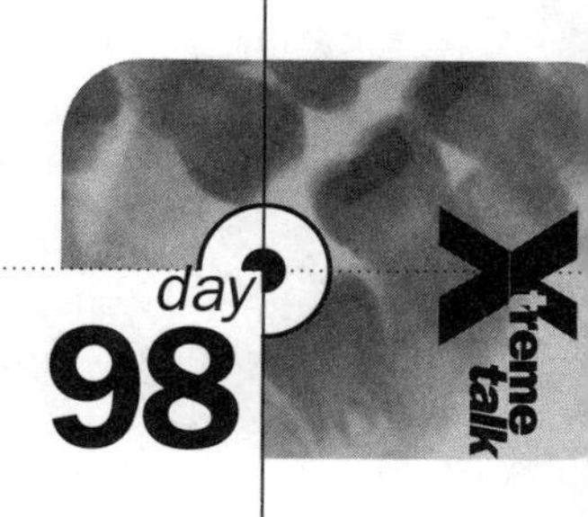

what good does it do to be patient?

James 1:4 says that patience produces maturity. When you are patient, your relationships become a lot more peaceful and last a whole lot longer.

Look at how it worked in Jesus' life. He had twelve friends who stuck with Him through thick and thin, and He was the perfect portrayal of patience. For instance, I can't imagine Jesus ever losing His temper and yelling at Peter. Maybe Jesus felt like yelling at times, but He didn't because this quality of patience had been developed in Him.

Dear brothers, is your life full of difficulties and temptations? Then be happy, for when the way is rough, your patience has a chance to grow. So let it grow, and don't try to squirm out of your problems. For when your patience is finally in full bloom, then you will be ready for anything, strong in character, full and complete. — James 1:2-4 TLB

What about you? Are you able to keep your cool when everyone else around you loses theirs? Patience may be the answer you've been looking for.

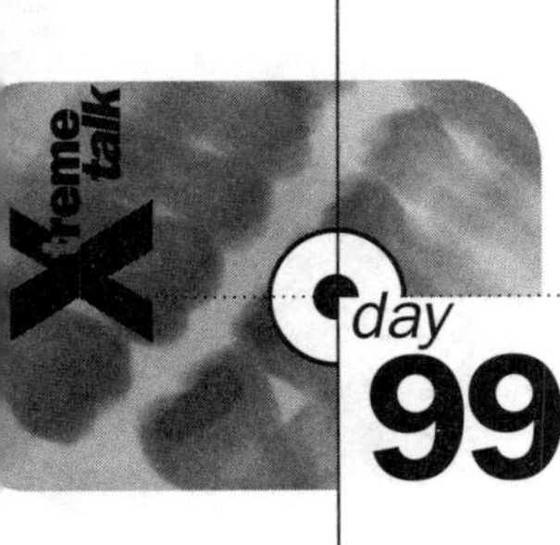

how can I improve my communication with others so there isn't any misunderstanding?

So many things can go wrong when we don't communicate accurately with each other. But we need to realize that misunderstandings are going to happen. They are nothing to get upset about.

The problem comes when we jump to conclusions and refuse to think the best about others. When we get ahead of the Holy Spirit — when we stop believing that God is in control and start letting worry and strife take over — the result is never good.

Agree with each other, love each other, be deep-spirited friends. Don't push your way to the front; don't sweet-talk your way to the top. Put yourself aside, and help others get ahead. Don't be obsessed with getting your own advantage. Forget yourselves long enough to lend a helping hand. — Philippians 2:2-4 THE MESSAGE

One way we can eliminate the misunderstandings is to get our mind saturated with God's Word so we can begin to act as Jesus acted. We can also check our motives to see that what we are doing and saying is coming from a pure heart.

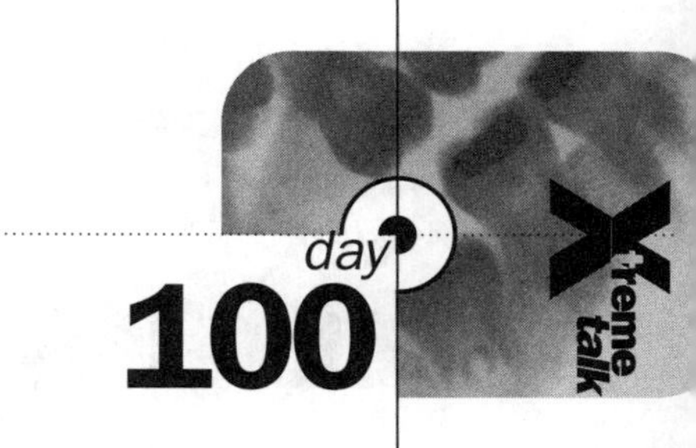

is it important to be accountable to friends?

Accountability to our Christian friends is absolutely vital to our spiritual walk. We all need friends who can ask tough questions about our actions and our thought life. These are the kinds of people who will give us advice straight out of God's Word and pray for us at a moment's notice.

If you don't have a friend like this in your life, pray and ask God to bring someone like that across your path.

Don't fool yourself into thinking that you are a listener when you are anything but, letting the Word go in one ear and out the other. Act on what you hear! Those who hear and don't act are like those who glance in the mirror, walk away, and two minutes later have no idea who they are, what they look like. — James 1:22-24 THE MESSAGE

Just think about it this way: Your friends are like a mirror for you. They will reflect your character. If you don't know what you look like, how do you know what needs to be adjusted? You need people like this in your life who will be honest and true. You need good accountability mirrors.

why is being saved so important?

Have you ever wondered why salvation is a part of your spiritual armor? Ephesians 6:17 talks about your salvation being a *helmet* for you. A helmet guards your head. That's a very important part of your body to protect, since it makes every decision and regulates the functions of your body.

When you get saved, your salvation protects your mind, thoughts and decisions from all the devil's torment. This keeps you from going out on the spiritual battleground unprotected.

Take the helmet of salvation and the sword of the Spirit, which is the word of God. And pray in the Spirit on all occasions with all kinds of prayers and requests. With this in mind, be alert and always keep on praying for all the saints. — Ephesians 6:17,18 NIV

You are the one who chooses to put on your spiritual armor. So when you go to school, make sure you go armed and dangerous — *dangerous* against the devil and *armed* with the presence of God!

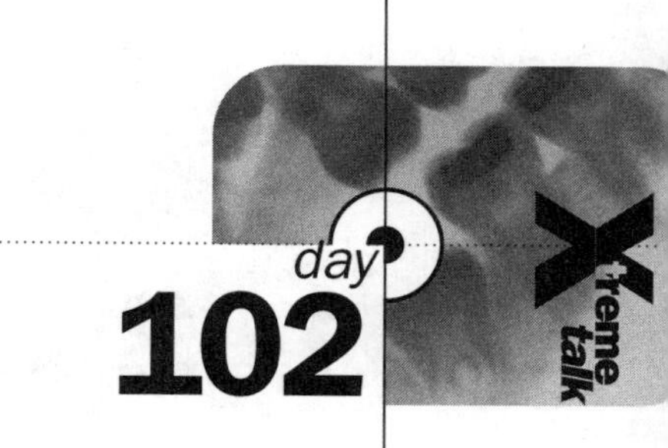

what is the breastplate of righteousness?

A lot of people wonder what righteousness means. It is just knowing that your relationship with God is one hundred percent right with no snags or grudges.

The Bible talks about righteousness as being a breastplate on a suit of armor. It is your modern-day, invisible "bullet-proof vest."

The devil will do his best to aim where he thinks he can kill you — in those vulnerable areas of your life where you are most likely to be wounded.

When Christians see the enemy's arrows coming at them, too many times they give up and hit the deck. They doubt that their relationship with the Lord is strong enough to withstand the attack because they aren't totally convinced that they are standing right with Him. They forget all about their "bullet-proof vest" of righteousness.

Stand firm then, with the belt of truth buckled around your waist, with the breastplate of righteousness in place, and with your feet fitted with the readiness that comes from the gospel of peace. — Ephesians 6:14,15 **NIV**

As children of God, we can stand up to those puny little arrows the devil throws our way. Nothing can harm us when we know that God will honor our right relationship with Him.

where do you really find the truth about things?

Ephesians 6 lists the belt of truth as a part of the armor of God. It is what holds everything together. In the same way, we need to clothe ourselves with the truth found in God's Word.

How can we effectively fight any battle if we are always worried about "losing our trousers" in a spiritual discussion with our peers?

When we go to our school ready to do battle for the Lord, we have to have some of the basic issues of our faith settled in stone. Those issues have to be true to us, or we will be worried in every scuffle about exposing our own uncertainties. We need to focus on the specific challenge before us without having to worry about whether or not what we believe is true.

Stand firm then, with the belt of truth buckled around your waist, with the breastplate of righteousness in place, and with your feet fitted with the readiness that comes from the gospel of peace. — Ephesians 6:14,15 NIV

So arm yourself with the belt of truth, and you will be confident in every situation.

what is the shield of faith?

When the Bible says to arm ourselves with the shield of faith, it isn't talking about some space-invader force field that magically appears around us. The shield of faith is something that we have to make a decision to pick up every day of our lives. We have the ability to block every fiery dart the Bible warns us about.

You see, just because we have faith doesn't mean that Satan won't try to hurl some nasty darts at us. But if we know how to block each one, we will be armed and dangerous against the devil.

For example, when fiery darts of depression come at us, we can pick up our shield of faith and say, "The joy of the Lord is my strength." Boom! That attack of the enemy is blocked. Or when fiery darts of sickness come our way, we can pick up that invisible shield and say, "By His stripes I am healed."

In addition to all this, take up the shield of faith, with which you can extinguish all the flaming arrows of the evil one. — Ephesians 6:16 NIV

Your shield of faith comes by hearing the Word of God and believing it is true. So take up your shield of faith, and win the victory!

what is the sword of the Spirit?

The one offensive weapon in Ephesians 6 is the sword of the Spirit. Everything else in the armor of God helps you stand your ground, but your sword helps you advance against the enemy.

According to this verse, the sword of the Spirit is the Word of God. Jesus used that spiritual weapon against the devil, saying, "It is written...." You can do the same thing.

The truth is, you can't go into battle and win without the sword of the Spirit. No matter how skilled you are at arguing the gospel of Jesus Christ, you will never effectively advance God's kingdom until people see the power of God's Word and the evidence of the Holy Spirit in your life.

Winning your friends to Christ and standing strong against the devil doesn't have to be such a struggle. The Holy Spirit lives in you, and, as you wield the sword of God's Word, He will fight every single battle for you.

Take the helmet of salvation and the sword of the Spirit, which is the word of God. — Ephesians 6:17 NIV

When people see the power of the Word and the Holy Spirit in your life, the callused layers surrounding their hearts will just melt away. The love of Jesus reflected in you will win them over to Him.

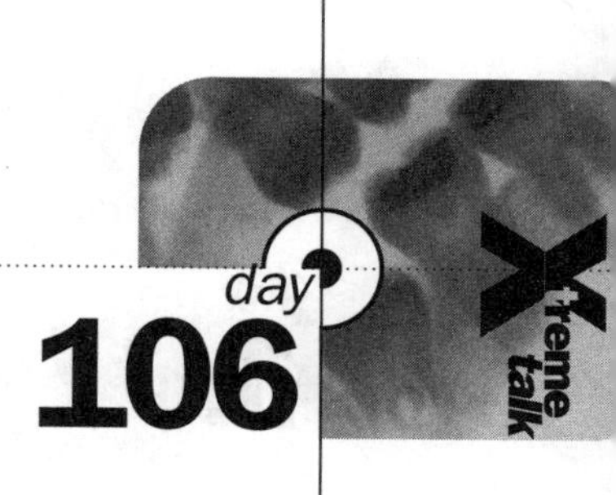

day
106

where can I find opportunities to tell people about Jesus?

If you want to have tons of opportunities to tell people about Jesus at your school, just get involved in some extracurricular activities. After-school activities introduce you to a bunch of new people and give you a great springboard for friendships because you usually have things in common with each other.

It is good to stretch your comfort zones, and getting involved with new people will help you do that. Developing new relationships keeps you growing and changing and prevents you from becoming too complacent.

It's news I'm most proud to proclaim, this extraordinary Message of God's powerful plan to rescue everyone who trusts him, starting with Jews and then right on to everyone else! — Romans 1:16 THE MESSAGE

Go ahead — take a step of obedience and get involved in some extracurricular activities. Don't do it because everybody else is doing it, but because you need to stretch yourself. Rise to the challenge, and increase your circle of influence.

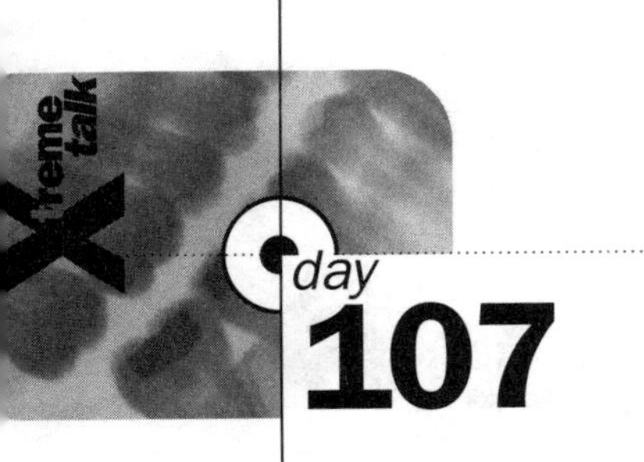

why be positive toward teachers when it isn't always popular to do that?

You may not believe this, but your teachers are not a tool designed by Satan to make your life miserable. In fact, many of them need Jesus too.

Sometimes it is easy for you as a teenager to forget that your teachers are just people. Teachers have hopes and dreams. Many of them have family problems, and they wonder about God just like you do.

You may think that your teachers would never listen to you if you tried to share the love of Jesus with them, but that isn't true. The key is to build a healthy relationship with them so they *will* listen. Be respectful and kind, and they will see that there is more to you than just another face in class.

Get the word out. Teach all these things. And don't let anyone put you down because you're young. Teach believers with your life: by word, by demeanor, by love, by faith, by integrity. Stay at your post reading Scripture, giving counsel, teaching. And that special gift of ministry you were given when the leaders of the church laid hands on you and prayed — keep that dusted off and in use. — 1 Timothy 4:11-14 THE MESSAGE

Just follow the counsel of First Timothy 4:12 NIV: **Don't let anyone look down on you because you are young, but set an example.** Someday you will wish you had the opportunity to impact some of the most influential people in our nation — our educators — so make the most of the opportunity you have with your teachers today.

can too much procrastination in your life ruin it?

Procrastination can seem like such an innocent character flaw. After all, it is just creatively wasting time, isn't it? But, actually, procrastination really has its roots in fear and laziness, and those are two weaknesses that can ruin you.

Proverbs 12:24 NIV says that **laziness ends in slave labor.** Does that sound like fun to you? Of course not. Laziness is slavery and bondage to your flesh. It is a waste of both yours and other people's time — time that could be spent advancing the kingdom of God.

But make sure that you don't get so absorbed and exhausted in taking care of all your day-by-day obligations that you lose track of the time and doze off, oblivious to God. The night is about over, dawn is about to break. Be up and awake to what God is doing! — Romans 13:11 THE MESSAGE

As a Christian, you have been given a challenge in Romans 13:11 to understand this present time and to *wake up* from your spiritual slumber. So don't let yourself develop bad habits of procrastination. Be diligent in all things, and make room for God's timetable in your agenda. The hour has come. It is time for action!

how do I obtain the favor of God in my life?

At times we all have a tendency to worry about getting along with other people and making friends. But I have some good news for you. If you believe the Bible (and I know you do), then you have a promise in Psalm 5:12 that you can hold on to. This verse says that God will surround His righteous ones with favor like a shield.

Whoa, what a promise! With that promise to claim as your own, what do you have to worry about? God wants to help you make the most out of every opportunity. He does that by surrounding you with His supernatural favor, no matter where you are or what you are doing.

But let all who take refuge in you be glad; let them ever sing for joy. Spread your protection over them, that those who love your name may rejoice in you. For surely, O Lord, you bless the righteous; you surround them with your favor as with a shield. — Psalm 5:11,12 NIV

When you diligently seek the Lord, you begin to experience His favor like never before. In fact, God wants you to experience His favor in an even greater way than you are right now. So trust Him with every part of your life, and watch His favor surround you like a shield.

why is it important to pray about which college I should attend?

God has some big plans for your life. In fact, the Bible says that your steps are ordered by the Lord. (Psalm 37:23.) Surely that means He will help you decide on a college to go to. The question is, are you willing to submit your choice to His will?

It's not hard to submit to God's will once you understand that He wants only the best for you. He wants you to maximize your opportunity for an education so you can walk out the plan He has ordained for your life.

Now that I'm separated from you, keep it up. Better yet, redouble your efforts. Be energetic in your life of salvation, reverent and sensitive before God. That energy is God's energy, an energy deep within you, God himself willing and working at what will give him the most pleasure.
— Philippians 2:12-13 THE MESSAGE

God puts His ability and His desires in you. He will lead you to the college that best fits into His ultimate design for you. It will be the college that can best equip you for the ministry opportunities God has called you to fulfill. That's why Jesus wants to be Lord of all your decisions — including the important decision of where to attend college.

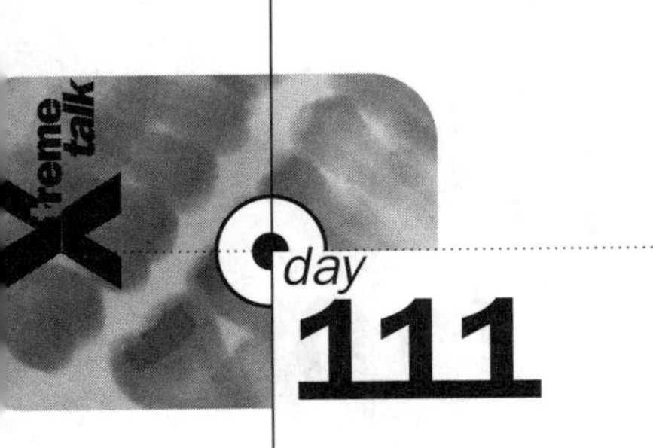

how can I improve my memory and study habits?

This one is for all you overachievers out there: God should be higher in priority than your grades!

It may not seem like it, but grades can become a god if you become consumed with them. So if an intense drive for achievement and success controls you, you need to make some adjustments.

First, you need to make sure you are spending quality time with God every single day. Bring to His throne your desire to make good grades, and ask the Holy Spirit to honor that desire. If you will be faithful in your quiet times and humble enough to admit that you can't succeed without the Lord's help anyway, He will honor your diligence.

But seek first his kingdom and his righteousness, and all these things will be given to you as well. Therefore do not worry about tomorrow, for tomorrow will worry about itself. Each day has enough trouble of its own. — Matthew 6:33,34 NIV

You don't have to get good grades at the expense of a relationship with your heavenly Father. Put in the time with Him, and He will multiply back to you the time and effort you spend studying.

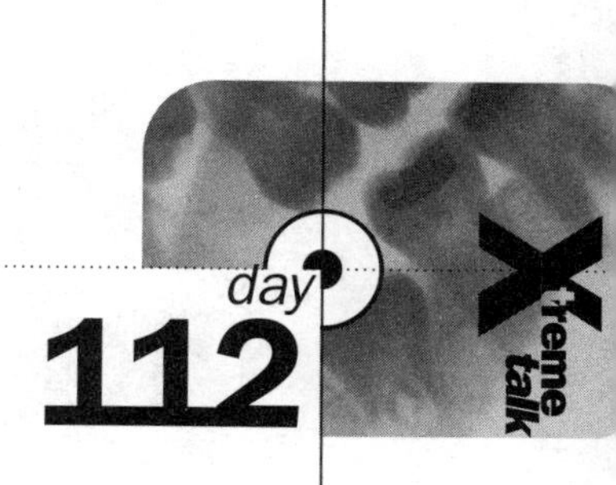

how can God help me with my study habits in school?

God honors diligence. Most of the time we want to make good grades, but the problem comes when we have to actually sit down and study to make it happen. I know — I have been there. The spirit is willing, but the flesh is weak.

If you lack the discipline to really buckle down and do your schoolwork, you need to make some corrections in your life. You don't necessarily have a discipline problem; you might have a *vision* problem.

Therefore, the first thing you have to do is to get a vision of your success in school. See yourself doing well with the schoolwork assigned to you. Then be sure to keep up your personal time with God. Remind God every day about what His Word says concerning studying. For instance, First Corinthians 2:16 says that you have the mind of Christ.

Finally, you need to provide yourself with a good environment to study in. That definitely does *not* mean sitting in front of a TV!

The spiritual man makes judgments about all things, but he himself is not subject to any man's judgment: "For who has known the mind of the Lord that he may instruct him?" But we have the mind of Christ.
— 1 Corinthians 2:15,16 NIV

If you will do your part, God will do His to help you develop good study habits. Remember, He always honors diligence.

day
113

how important are goals in your life?

Goal-setting is one of the most important things you can do to stay on track with your schoolwork. As the saying goes, if you *fail to plan,* you *plan to fail.*

What kind of goals are you setting for your academic success? If you don't expect too much of yourself, you will never excel in anything.

Proverbs 16:3 says that if you commit to the Lord everything you do, your plans will succeed. That means you have to plan to begin with.

So when you are striving for a goal such as getting term papers in on time, scoring well on tests or pulling up your GPA, ask the Lord to help you become more effective. He will honor your diligence.

Commit to the Lord whatever you do, and your plans will succeed.
— Proverbs 16:3 NIV

God wants you to fulfill your potential. But in order to do that, you will have to first set goals for yourself and then determine to reach them by God's grace.

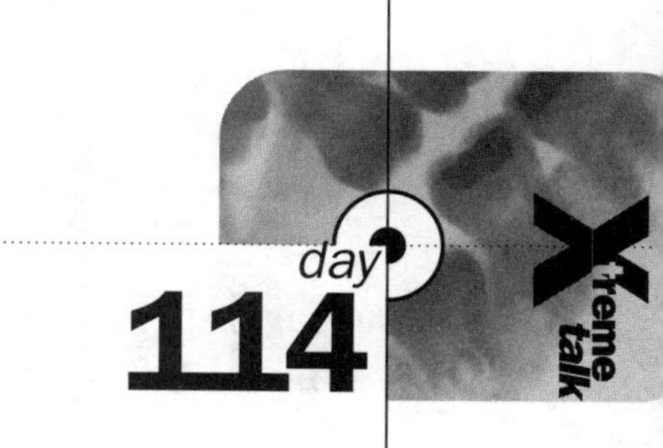

how can I get my priorities straight?

It is easy to say, "I don't have enough time." But I have found out that you can make time for just about anything in your life if you really try. However, it *is* true that you can't do everything. That's why you need to prioritize.

We waste so much time doing things that aren't necessarily important; meanwhile, other more important things seem to get neglected.

So keep in mind when you are prioritizing that what you want to do may not necessarily be the most important things to do. For example, you may want to go to the movies instead of doing your algebra homework. But if you start flunking algebra, suddenly doing your homework becomes a much higher priority than going to the movies.

Trust in the Lord with all your heart and lean not on your own understanding; in all your ways acknowledge him, and he will make your paths straight. — Proverbs 3:5,6 NIV

Setting priorities sometimes means dying to your flesh. But in the end, it will all be worth it, because the things in life that are most important will finally have your attention.

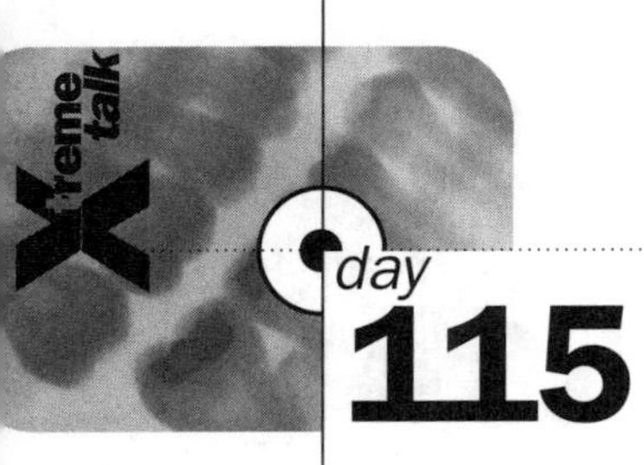

day
115

what does the Bible say about prejudice?

As much as we may hate prejudice, God hates it even more. Unfortunately for many people, prejudice is a reality of everyday life. Whether it is racism, sexism or any other kind of "ism," it is never pleasing to the Lord.

One of the most important commandments God gave us is to love our neighbors as we love yourselves. It's wrong to pass judgment on someone because you possess a limited amount of knowledge that applies to just a few people in a particular group. When you stereotype someone because of his or her race, gender, color, social standing or anything else, you just aren't being fair. To truly love your neighbor, you will have to set aside your prejudices and stereotypes.

What if you become a victim of prejudice yourself? You will have to demonstrate love to your neighbor. The Bible gives you no right to be a defensive victim. You, and you alone, are responsible for your reactions to every injustice, so make sure those reactions are honorable.

He answered: "'Love the Lord your God with all your heart and with all your soul and with all your strength and with all your mind'; and, 'Love your neighbor as yourself.'" — Luke 10:27 NIV

Prejudice only ends up dividing people and causing strife. We as Christians must overcome evil with good by loving our neighbor as ourselves.

why are theories stressed in the science texts as being the truth?

Evolution has been a hot topic in public schools for years. As a matter of fact, you may have even been engulfed in heated conversations about it in your own classes at school. However, arguments and insults about what other people think never honor God. Besides, it is difficult for anyone who doesn't know the Creator to see His creation in its truest light.

Try to look at it from this perspective: Showing people how much they need Jesus should take first priority over showing them why your side of the evolution argument is right. I know it can be a bummer to have your own teachers and friends deny the fundamental truths that you find basic to your faith in God. But face the evolution issue the same way you would any other kind of persecution: with joy and with boldness. Don't be so defensive. You know the truth.

Don't have anything to do with foolish and stupid arguments, because you know they produce quarrels. — 2 Timothy 2:23 NIV

It's like my buddy Geoff Moore says, "Evolution is the changing of the heart and the renewing of the mind."

day
117

I am in a group of friends who are really tight. is there anything wrong with that?

I realize that cliques are a part of today's schools and youth groups. After all, doesn't it make sense that "birds of a feather flock together"? But cliques can be a very destructive part of life because they leave people out and hurt people's feelings. Someday, sooner or later, you will probably be one of those people.

You may be part of a clique without even realizing it. Think about this. When was the last time you were told *not* to invite someone whom you knew wanted to hang out with you just because that person wasn't a part of your circle of friends?

Do nothing out of selfish ambition or vain conceit, but in humility consider others better than yourselves. Each of you should look not only to your own interests, but also to the interests of others. — Philippians 2:3,4 NIV

The next time that happens, take a step to prove God's unconditional love and reach out to someone who may not feel as if he or she is a part of your group. That one simple act could really minister to that person. God honors those who are generous, especially with their friendship.

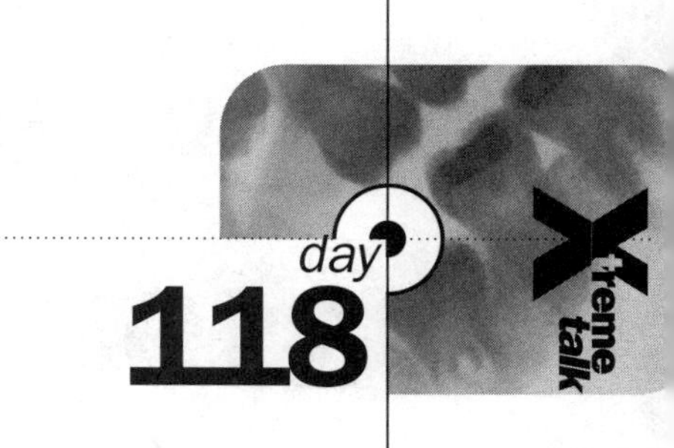

why does fear seem to keep me from moving ahead?

Whenever you start to feel nervous or afraid of anything, you can save yourself a lot of time wondering if God is in the situation by knowing that fear is never from God. The only good fear is the fear (or the reverence) of the Lord.

The Word says that God has not given us the spirit of fear, but of power, love and a sound mind. (2 Timothy 1:7.) It is the devil that brings fear of what others think about you. He wants you to believe that you aren't cool if you follow Christ.

Be strong and courageous. Do not be afraid or terrified because of them, for the Lord your God goes with you; he will never leave you nor forsake you." — Deuteronomy 31:6 **NIV**

So be strong and take courage, for God is with you always.

why is there persecution in the world?

In Jesus, we have complete and total victory over any attack of the devil. But even if we are totally following God, we are almost guaranteed one hardship: the persecution of our faith.

No one understood this better than Paul the apostle. Even in the midst of jail and the promise of almost certain death, he remained joyful that he could serve the Lord until the end.

Paul wrote Philippians 1:19 from prison, saying, “Yes, I’ll continue to rejoice, for I know that through your prayers and the help given by the Spirit, what has happened to me will turn out for my deliverance.” Whoa, what an attitude!

***Yes, and I will continue to rejoice, for I know that through your prayers and the help given by the Spirit of Jesus Christ, what has happened to me will turn out for my deliverance. I eagerly expect and hope that I will in no way be ashamed, but will have sufficient courage so that now as always Christ will be exalted in my body, whether by life or by death. For to me, to live is Christ and to die is gain. — Philippians 1:18-21* NIV**

So the next time you feel persecuted or treated unfairly for being a Christian, just go ahead and make a conscious effort to rejoice. You can’t control others’ actions, so you may as well control your own reactions!

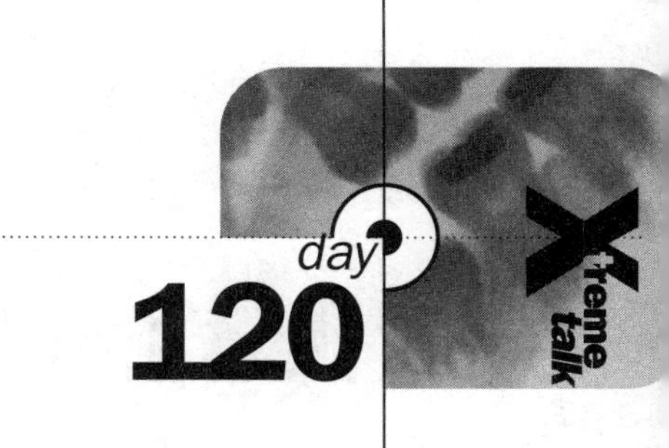

why are so many girls in my school getting pregnant?

There is a lot of compromise in the world, and sometimes it is easy to blur lines and confuse issues. But I will tell you this — it isn't a pregnancy issue that we need to be concerned about. It is a *sin* issue.

When a teenage girl gets pregnant, it is only a symptom of the sin of premarital sex. This happens when teenagers don't fully understand or care about what God's Word says on the subject of waiting until marriage for sex.

As Christians, we should show God's love to our friends who are dealing with pregnancy. We need to let them know that God isn't mad at them. In fact, His desire for them is to accept the forgiveness that comes through Jesus.

Live creatively, friends. If someone falls into sin, forgivingly restore him, saving your critical comments for yourself. You might be needing forgiveness before the day's out. Stoop down and reach out to those who are oppressed. Share their burdens, and so complete Christ's law. If you think you are too good for that, you are badly deceived. — Galatians 6:1-3 THE MESSAGE

As for ourselves, we need to meditate on how much God has done for us. When we truly understand that, we will *want* to live a pure life.

why do people hate others based on their color?

It is amazing to me to see how far our society has come in the struggle against racism. But the truth is, a lot of people still struggle with this problem. Although some people have never had to deal with racism, other people seem to deal with it on a regular basis.

As Christians, we need to look for ways to overcome racism. But first, it's important to realize that this isn't a new issue.

When Jesus told the story of the Good Samaritan in Luke 10, He was giving us a lesson that can be applied to all situations involving racism. The bottom line is this: Consider others as you would consider yourself.

If you have any encouragement from being united with Christ, if any comfort from his love, if any fellowship with the Spirit, if any tenderness and compassion, then make my joy complete by being like-minded, having the same love, being one in spirit and purpose. Do nothing out of selfish ambition or vain conceit, but in humility consider others better than yourselves. Each of you should look not only to your own interests, but also to the interests of others. — Philippians 2:1-4 NIV

Now, if you are a victim of racism, remember that God's love in you can cover a multitude of sins. But if you have been guilty of racism, it is important that you repent and ask God to help you love others just as you love yourself. It is God's desire for you to live in unity with other people, regardless of their race or color.

seeking a natural "high" is only a temporary experience. so what does it mean to experience a "high" from God?

I can't believe some of the wild things people do just for thrills. There is no doubt about it — this generation is labeled as extreme. Now, there is nothing necessarily wrong with thrill-seeking, but let's look at the reason why a lot of people go to extremes just to experience a temporary adrenaline high.

Our culture and technology are so advanced. We have a lot more experiences through which we can look at life. Therefore, we try to invent new and creative ways to satisfy our need for excitement.

But people miss the plain and simple fact that nothing will satisfy them *except* the love of God. No bungee dive or drug could top that!

Your attitude should be the same as that of Christ Jesus: Who, being in very nature God, did not consider equality with God something to be grasped, but made himself nothing, taking the very nature of a servant, being made in human likeness. — Philippians 2:5-7 NIV

Imagine for a moment the Creator of the universe. He existed before the universe was, and He is the Mastermind behind all its activity. Imagine now that this same Creator can actually live in our finite human hearts and pour out His love through us. Now *that* is extreme!

homosexuality is wrong. why are schools so open to it?

Nowadays our society has taken a "to-each-his-own" stance regarding homosexuality in an effort not to offend anyone. Homosexuality is in the process of becoming widely accepted and is even being taught as a "lifestyle option." Some curriculum is even introducing it in the classroom, encouraging students to explore it!

But God *never* calls this lifestyle an option. He calls it *sin.* So how do you deal with the fact that one or more of your friends at school may be professing homosexuals?

Well, first of all, if you are ever going to be able to help those friends, you must have a voice in their lives. This means they need to respect your influence. But that will never happen if you join others in harassing them.

Just like you, these friends need God's love. Remember, however, that they are bound with a strong deception, and their only hope for freedom is through Jesus.

Also, here's a very important point to remember: Because homosexuality is such a strong deception, be sure to keep yourself accountable to your Christian friends when you do reach out to any teens who claim to be homosexual. There is always the possibility that they may try to pull you in.

Do you not know that the wicked will not inherit the kingdom of God? Do not be deceived: Neither the sexually immoral nor idolaters nor adulterers nor male prostitutes nor homosexual offenders....And that is what some of you were. But you were washed, you were sanctified, you were justified in the name of the Lord Jesus Christ and by the Spirit of our God. — 1 Corinthians 6:9-11 **NIV**

Finally, understand that you don't have to love these people's sin, but God has called you to love *them.* You *can* make a difference in their lives.

how important is it that I find out what God has called me to do?

You know, the mentality of living for the moment robs people today of a sense of destiny.

But you weren't put here just to collect momentary memories. You were created for a purpose. Did you know that God has already thought out that purpose in detail? He has a plan for your life. In fact, Jeremiah 29:11 says that in Him you have a future and a hope!

"For I know the plans I have for you," declares the Lord, "plans to prosper you and not to harm you, plans to give you hope and a future. Then you will call upon me and come and pray to me, and I will listen to you. You will seek me and find me when you seek me with all your heart. I will be found by you," declares the Lord, "and will bring you back from captivity." — Jeremiah 29:11-14 NIV

I don't care what you have been taught before — life isn't an accident. *You* aren't an accident. There are some things that God wants to accomplish here on earth in your lifetime that only you can do. You have a destiny, and He will equip you to fulfill it.

I have a big problem with people who brag about themselves. how do I keep from making the same mistake?

You have probably met people who seem to go on and on and on about themselves. Who knows, you may even be one of those people. But excessive bragging stems from insecurity.

If someone is speaking about something that you are pretty good at, do you always feel that you have to tell more about yourself? For instance, what about spiritual things? Are you constantly letting other people know how many Bible chapters you have read or how long you pray?

Young men, in the same way be submissive to those who are older. All of you, clothe yourselves with humility toward one another, because, "God opposes the proud but gives grace to the humble." Humble yourselves, therefore, under God's mighty hand, that he may lift you up in due time. Cast all your anxiety on him because he cares for you. — 1 Peter 5:5-7 NIV

Jesus said in Matthew 6:1 that we need to be careful not to let our acts of righteousness be done before men just to be seen by them. If we do, we will have no reward from our Father in heaven. We need to walk humbly, make sure our security is in Jesus and be careful not to brag.

can people who sometimes get angry be pleasing God?

You are only human, right? So if you lash out occasionally at others in anger, that's okay. Bzzzzzt! Wrong answer. I wonder what Jesus would say about that kind of reasoning? Well, in Matthew 5:22 He says that anyone who is angry with his brother without a cause is subject to judgment.

According to this Scripture, there is such a thing as being angry for a righteous cause. Remember how Jesus responded when He saw people in the temple selling sacrifices to make money? He became very angry and turned over the moneychangers' tables — yet the Bible says Jesus lived a life without sin. I believe, however, that when Jesus got angry, He was in control of His anger; *it* wasn't in control of *Him.*

But this is where some of us miss it. We get upset about something, and then instead of staying in control of our emotions, we allow our anger to control *us.* Sometimes we even lash out at people in an uncontrolled rage. This fleshly display of anger is destructive and usually ends up hurting people.

Ephesians 4:26 says, **Be ye angry, and sin not: let not the sun go down upon your wrath: Neither give place to the devil.** So according to this verse, anger does happen. It is like a warning flag telling us that we have been crossed or violated in some way.

When we feel angry, we need to take note of what has happened to make us feel that way and then address the problem before it happens again. The Bible says we are to deal with whatever has made us angry before the sun goes down. That way it has less opportunity to build up and explode on the inside of us.

If you have a difficult time controlling your temper and you believe that you can do nothing about it, then you have fallen for a lie from Satan himself. The truth is, anger is a learned behavior, and it *can* be controlled.

***"In your anger do not sin": Do not let the sun go down while you are still angry, and do not give the devil a foothold. — Ephesians 4:26-27* NIV**

So let your mind become renewed by the Word of God. Believe and confess today that you are free from uncontrolled anger that leads to sin.

how can I tell if I have allowed jealousy to take root in my life?

Jealousy is something we all have to face at some point in our lives. But some people let jealousy take root in their heart, allowing it to become an actual part of their personality. What a miserable life that would be — always looking to see what other people get, then becoming jealous and resentful when they get it!

We can all find something to be jealous about if we look at other people's lives hard enough. The key to ending jealousy in our lives isn't to become the best at every endeavor or to have the best of every possession; it is to learn how to be *thankful* for who we are and what we already have in Jesus Christ.

For where you have envy and selfish ambition, there you find disorder and every evil practice. — James 3:16 NIV

In fact, the Bible says you are *complete* in Christ. (Colossians 2:10.) When that truth becomes a revelation in your heart, jealousy won't be a problem for you anymore.

day
128

how important is it to balance my time between talking and listening?

People who talk too much are probably not even aware that they do it. Most of the time this habit is purely innocent.

In your own life, be careful about developing an unhealthy need for attention — especially if you are known for your many words. Learning to get a grip on your tongue and to keep yourself from talking too much will take you far and win you favor.

When words are many, sin is not absent, but he who holds his tongue is wise. — Proverbs 10:19 NIV

So remember, the best way to make friends is not to do all the talking yourself but to be a good listener.

how can laziness destroy my life?

Laziness is more than a bad habit. It has the potential to poison every part of your life, from school to work to your relationships. Laziness can actually become ingrained in your personality.

It is safe to say that if you let discipline slip in one area of your life, it will eventually slip in other areas as well. Just look around you. Is your room cluttered? Are your parents always having to ride you about getting your chores done?

Lazy hands make a man poor, but diligent hands bring wealth.
— Proverbs 10:4 NIV

If you don't get a hold on your lack of self-discipline, laziness will eventually get a hold on you. Proverbs 10:4 says that lazy hands make a man poor. Now, that doesn't make a life of laziness sound too appealing, does it?

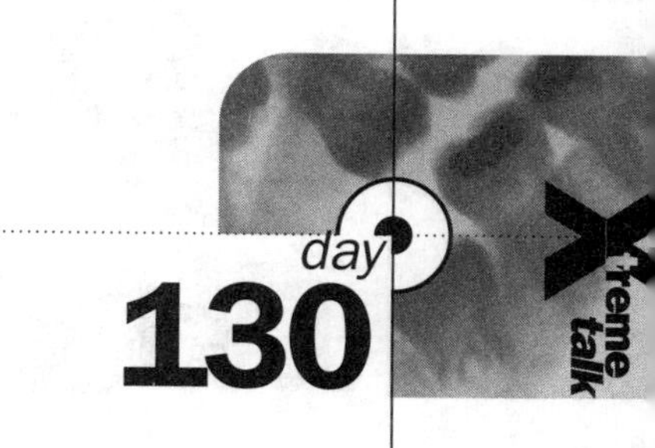

what can I do to keep my thoughts pure?

Do you know that your thought life doesn't just pertain to impure sexual thoughts? Wrong thoughts can include the negative way you think about yourself and about others. They can also include worries, doubts and fears. You see, although your spirit is made new when you are born again, your mind remains the same and must be renewed by feeding on the Word of God.

Second Corinthians 10:5 says that you should take every thought captive and make it obedient to Christ. Does that verse really mean *every* thought? Yes, it sure does.

One way you can capture these thoughts is by meditating on the Word of God ahead of time. That way when thoughts contrary to God's Word enter your mind, you will be able to recognize them for what they are, take them out back and shoot them with the gospel gun!

It doesn't happen all at once, but over a period of time your thoughts will begin to change. More and more you will think thoughts that are in line with the way Jesus thinks.

Summing it all up, friends, I'd say you'll do best by filling your minds and meditating on things true, noble, reputable, authentic, compelling, gracious — the best, not the worst; the beautiful, not the ugly; things to praise, not things to curse. Put into practice what you learned from me, what you heard and saw and realized. Do that, and God, who makes everything work together, will work you into his most excellent harmonies. — Philippians 4:8,9 **THE MESSAGE**

Eventually those thoughts will begin to affect your actions as well. You will find yourself making different, more godly choices than you would have made in the past. In time, you will look back and see the great difference that God's Word has made in your life. Because you were faithful to renew your mind with the Word, you will never be the same again.

where does confusion come from?

Confusion is never from God. In fact, He has promised to order your steps. (Psalm 37:23.) One way you can win the battle over confusion in your life is to simply stop confessing that you are confused.

Have you ever heard yourself saying, "I'm so confused; I don't know what I'm going to do"? Well, of course you don't know what you are going to do when you keep speaking that kind of doubt. You need to begin to say what God's Word says about you: "I hear the voice of my Father, and the voice of a stranger I don't even recognize." (John 10:4,5.)

For God did not give us a spirit of timidity, but a spirit of power, of love and of self-discipline. — 2 Timothy 1:7 NIV

When you meditate on God's promises, confusion will fade away, and God will make your choices clear.

how can the root of bitterness stop the flow of God's love?

Each day you will have an opportunity to get offended. If you let offenses take root in your life, you will eventually become bitter toward various individuals and even life in general.

Jesus said that offenses would come. (Matthew 18:7.) When they do, you must walk right past them. You can't afford to pick up offenses and keep thinking about them. Nursing a grudge will only make you bitter, and soon everything the person who offended you does will annoy you.

Instead, why don't you just choose to let go of the offense? Be thankful that you escaped the bitterness that could have held you back. Forgive the person or persons who offended you, and move on to what God has for you.

***The words "it was credited to him" were written not for him alone, but also for us, to whom God will credit righteousness — for us who believe in him who raised Jesus our Lord from the dead. He was delivered over to death for our sins and was raised to life for our justification. — Romans 4:23-25* NIV**

Every time you let go of an offense, it builds your character. So choose to allow the offense to make you *better,* not *bitter.* Remember that God's blessings are far greater than any offense.

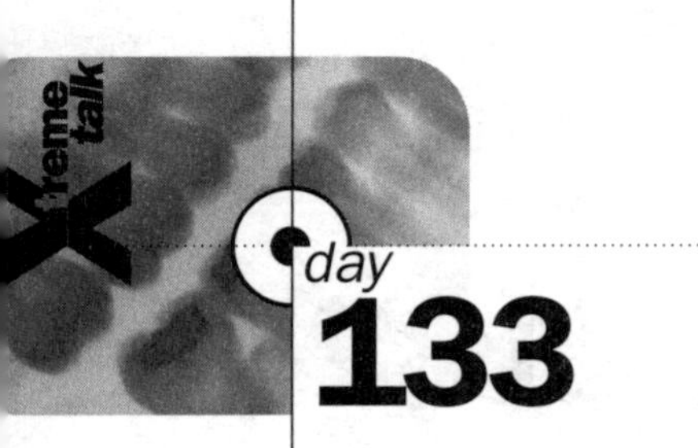

day
133

who tempts me, God or the devil?

Let's set the record straight. God isn't the One Who tempts you. James 1:13 says that God can't be tempted and that He can't tempt anyone else either. Temptation is clearly from the devil, who has no other purpose but to entice you into sin.

But don't worry. God has given you the power to say no in any situation. He will provide a way of escape in the middle of every temptation. (1 Corinthians 10:13.)

Don't let anyone under pressure to give in to evil say, "God is trying to trip me up." God is impervious to evil, and puts evil in no one's way. The temptation to give in to evil comes from us and only us. We have no one to blame but the leering, seducing flareup of our own lust. Lust gets pregnant, and has a baby: sin! Sin grows up to adulthood, and becomes a real killer. — James 1:13-15 THE MESSAGE

You can win the same way Jesus did. He used the Word and said, "It is written...." (Matthew 4:10.) If it worked for Jesus, it will work for you. The Word is your key to victory. Meditate on it, know it and live it.

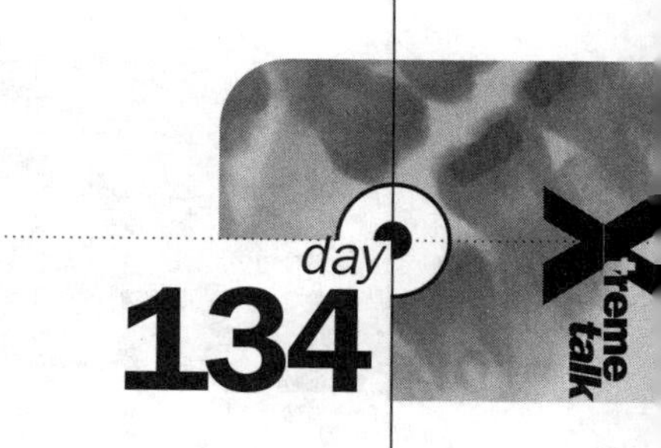

day
134

why is it so bad to worry?

Did you know that worry is a sin? The Bible says to be anxious for nothing, and that means *nothing*. When we pray about something, we are releasing it to God to take care of it. But then when we start to worry, we take the problem out of God's hands and put it back into our own. As a result, nothing productive comes from our prayer.

One of my friends put it this way: "Worry is a darkroom where negatives are developed." In other words, the more you think on the negative, the more pronounced and developed the negative will become.

If you worry a lot, begin to speak what God's Word says about you. Start saying, "I'm not anxious about anything. The peace of Christ guards my heart and mind." Replace the negative with the positive, and begin to move in a new direction.

And the peace of God, which transcends all understanding, will guard your hearts and your minds in Christ Jesus. — Philippians 4:6,7 NIV

Do not be anxious about anything, but in everything, by prayer and petition, with thanksgiving, present your requests to God.

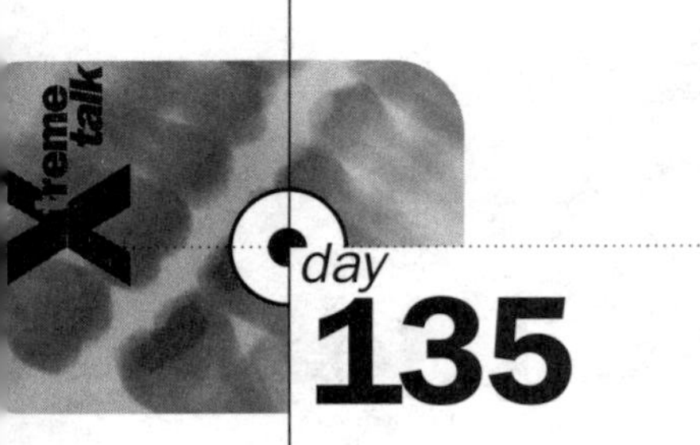

day

135

how can I know what is the right and wrong thing to do?

When someone makes an ethical decision, that means they make a decision based on their own understanding of what is right and wrong. But the problem is that everybody has a different perspective about what is right or wrong for his or her own life.

Every day we are faced with all kinds of ethical situations and questions. That is why we need the standard of God's Word and the leading of the Holy Spirit on the inside of us to show us what is right and wrong.

So if you are questioning what is the right or wrong thing for you to do, measure it up against God's Word. If God's Word says it is wrong, then don't do it. If God's Word doesn't directly talk about the situation you are facing, then look for a principle that fits what you are going through.

For there are three that testify: the Spirit, the water and the blood; and the three are in agreement. — 1 John 5:7,8 NIV

Otherwise, ask the Holy Spirit to help you, and He will guide you. He will never tell you to do anything that would contradict the Word because the Spirit and the Word always agree.

everything that comes on the tv is so negative and violent. what can I do about it?

So many people rip into the media, saying how biased and corrupt it is, and there is a lot of truth to that accusation. But I say that it is high time that we as Christians did something about it. If we aren't a part of the solution, then we are a part of the problem.

That is why our ministry designates so much of its budget to quality television and radio programming. Our goal is to provide programming that builds up people in Jesus and in the Word.

I have given them your word and the world has hated them, for they are not of the world any more than I am of the world. My prayer is not that you take them out of the world but that you protect them from the evil one. They are not of the world, even as I am not of it. Sanctify them by the truth; your word is truth. As you sent me into the world, I have sent them into the world. For them I sanctify myself, that they too may be truly sanctified. — John 17:14-19 **NIV**

But how can you as a teenager survive spiritually in a world full of negative media messages? Well, you can't live in a bubble the rest of your life, but you *can* be careful about what you hear and see, refusing to feed your mind with ungodly programs that grieve your spirit. You can also be a part of the solution by standing up and supporting the kind of television programming you believe in.

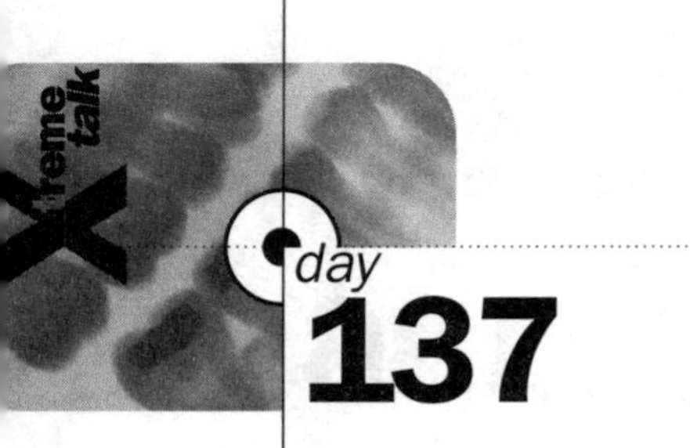

how can I know what is the right thing to do?

First of all, everybody has a conscience, and that conscience has a voice. We all recognize it, especially when we do something wrong. I call it the "right and wrong meter" on the inside.

Even when you aren't saved, your "right and wrong meter" still works. When you steal, it goes off on the inside and tells you that what you have just done is wrong. Then when you get saved, something powerful happens on the inside. Your "right and wrong meter" turns into a "better and best meter," and your standards of morality go to a whole new level.

As a teenager, you are going to have to learn how to resist the temptation of sins that others don't consider wrong. For example, a lot of people think that smoking dope isn't wrong, even though it is illegal. But you have a higher set of standards that keeps you from even considering the use of drugs.

Just because something is technically legal doesn't mean that it's spiritually appropriate. If I went around doing whatever I thought I could get by with, I'd be a slave to my whims.

You know the old saying, "First you eat to live, and then you live to eat"? Well, it may be true that the body is only a temporary thing, but that's no excuse for stuffing your body with food, or indulging it with sex. Since the Master honors you with a body, honor him with your body!
— 1 Corinthians 6:12,13 THE MESSAGE

Don't settle for just right or wrong. Let your morality be determined by the Holy Spirit in you. He will guide you to do the better and the best things that God has set forth in His Word.

how can I communicate more effectively?

Did you know that God wants to make you a good communicator? Just look at the example He set with His Son, Jesus.

Not only was Jesus a good Listener, but He also spoke with authority. That means He knew what He was talking about.

Well, if you are to survive in the real world, you will have to develop the same kind of good communication skills that Jesus had. When you know a lot about what you are talking about, it isn't hard to say it well because your words come from your heart.

***Watch the way you talk. Let nothing foul or dirty come out of your mouth. Say only what helps, each word a gift. — Ephesians 4:29* THE MESSAGE**

That's why, if you want to be able to effectively tell people about Jesus, you have to get to know Him by reading the Word and talking to Him in prayer. After a while, you will know what you are talking about, and it will come straight from your heart.

how much of the Bible should I study to be an effective Christian?

God's desire for you is to be so rock solid in Him that no amount of spiritual darkness can touch you. The Bible says that you are the light of the world and the salt of the earth. (Matthew 5:13,14.) Second Timothy 1:7 also says that God hasn't given you the spirit of fear, but of power, love and a sound mind.

According to these promises, you don't have to be afraid of the darkness by staying away from everybody who isn't a Christian. No way! You have what they need and what the devil is afraid of.

And I tell you that you are Peter, and on this rock I will build my church, and the gates of Hades will not overcome it. I will give you the keys of the kingdom of heaven; whatever you bind on earth will be bound in heaven, and whatever you loose on earth will be loosed in heaven.
— Matthew 16:18,19 NIV

But to be effective in reaching out to the lost, you have to study God's Word until it is planted deep on the inside of you. When you know God and His Word, you can have the confidence to invade the darkness because you know He is backing you up all the way!

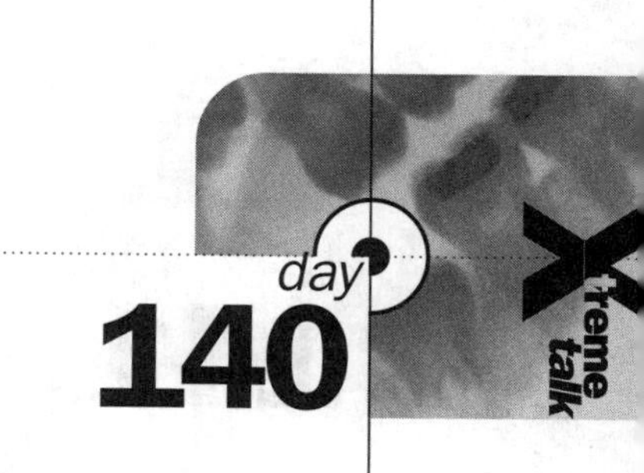

what is the word of wisdom?

A lot of Christians don't even know what the gifts of the Spirit are. (1 Corinthians 12:8-10.) As a result, they miss out on many of the blessings God wants them to experience.

One of these spiritual gifts is the word of wisdom. Often the word of wisdom will come into operation when you are in a situation where you don't know what to do or you aren't sure what is coming down the road.

It is at those times that the Holy Spirit may drop a specific piece of wisdom about that particular situation in your heart. This added information will help you make the right decision so you can do what is best.

The gifts of the Spirit are a tremendous aid to help you live your day-to-day life successfully. Sometimes when you say the word *Spirit,* people get spooked. But there really isn't anything to be spooked about. God loves you, and He wants you to walk in victory every single day of your life. Therefore, He has given you these gifts to help you along your way.

Which of you fathers, if your son asks for a fish, will give him a snake instead? Or if he asks for an egg, will give him a scorpion? If you then, though you are evil, know how to give good gifts to your children, how much more will your Father in heaven give the Holy Spirit to those who ask him! — Luke 11:11-13 NIV

If you want these spiritual gifts to operate in your life, you must first receive *the* Gift, the Holy Spirit. After you are filled with the Holy Spirit, ask Him to reveal Himself to you in a greater way. He will be faithful to do just that.

what is the word of knowledge?

Do you know that God loves you so much, He has given the gifts of the Holy Spirit to bless and encourage you? One of these gifts is the word of knowledge.

The word of knowledge is a word or insight about a situation that has already taken place or that is taking place right now. It usually provides you with knowledge about a situation that your mind knows nothing about.

Take, for example, a teenager just like you whose name is Jeremy. Out of the blue, he felt impressed that his friend Mark needed twenty dollars. This impression kept coming back to him throughout the day as he went about doing other things.

Now, as far as Jeremy knew, Mark was doing okay financially, but Jeremy gave his friend twenty dollars anyway. Later, he found out that Mark's wallet had been stolen the week before, along with twenty dollars that he needed for two weeks' worth of lunches.

Whoa! Was that a coincidence? No, Jeremy had a word of knowledge about Mark's need, and both of them grew in faith because of it.

***To one there is given through the Spirit the message of wisdom, to another the message of knowledge by means of the same Spirit.* — *1 Corinthians 12:8* NIV**

Sometimes the Holy Spirit may speak a very specific word of knowledge, or He may talk to you about a situation in general. Either way, the key is to be sure to listen to that supernatural knowledge and then to act on it in faith.

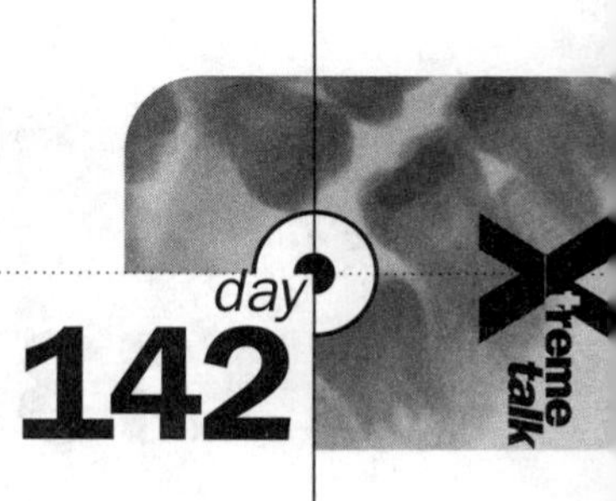

what is the gift of faith?

You have probably heard a lot about faith and how you need it for salvation, prayer and daily life. This kind of faith can be nurtured and fed so it will grow. It is something like a muscle; the more you use it, the stronger it will get. Faith moves the hand of God to work in certain situations.

However, the kind of faith Paul writes about in First Corinthians 12 is a little different. This faith is called *the gift of faith.* What is the difference?

The gift of faith is special because it goes beyond the faith you nurture and feed. This spiritual gift is reserved for needs in your life that require much more faith than what you may have at the time.

To another faith by the same Spirit, to another gifts of healing by that one Spirit. — 1 Corinthians 12:9 NIV

So when you don't have an ample supply of faith for a specific need, God in His mercy may grant you this extra dose of supernatural faith.

how important is it to be patient with others?

Every day each of us has an opportunity to be impatient. Most of us write our impatience off as a small character flaw. But patience is as important to our spiritual walk as it is to the relationships we have with others.

Impatience, which is the opposite of patience, shows up all the time in small ways. It is the angry comment you make in your car when you are in a hurry. It is the strained expression on your face when someone takes longer than you think they should. It is the intense tone of your voice when things don't go your way.

You might as well just relax, because half of what you think you need right now can wait. Besides, Romans 5 says that tribulations and trials in your life will help develop patience in your life.

Not only so, but we also rejoice in our sufferings, because we know that suffering produces perseverance; perseverance, character; and character, hope. And hope does not disappoint us, because God has poured out his love into our hearts by the Holy Spirit, whom he has given us. — Romans 5:3-5 NIV

So instead of trying to run from your trials, see if you can discover what God is trying to work inside of you. Then when you get through to the other side, you will be a more patient person for it.

what is the gift of prophecy?

God has given us the gift of prophecy to share with us *confirmation* about what is to come.

Suppose someone has what they believe is a word of prophecy for you. If after hearing the prophecy, you say, "Yeah, that's right! You are confirming in my heart what I already knew to be true," then it is probably a word from the Lord for you.

However, if the prophecy is something so far off the wall that it doesn't even sound familiar to you, then don't receive it. Either the person is speaking out of his human spirit, or he is spiritually off-base.

The Holy Spirit won't contradict Himself or confuse you. He is a Gentleman, and He won't tell you one thing and then have someone else tell you something different.

Now, the office of a prophet is different than just the simple gift of prophecy. A person with the gift of prophecy isn't necessarily a prophet, but the prophet always has the gift of prophecy in operation in his life. However, his prophetic words often have a greater element of foretelling in them.

To another miraculous powers, to another prophecy, to another distinguishing between spirits, to another speaking in different kinds of tongues, and to still another the interpretation of tongues. — 1 Corinthians 12:10 NIV

A prophetic message about things to come may not jump out and grab you because it may be speaking about matters you know nothing about. If you aren't sure about a prophecy that comes forth, it is best to set it on the shelf and see what God does with it. If it is from God, He will most surely bring it to pass.

if I think I have an eating disorder, what should I do?

When somebody develops an eating disorder such as anorexia or bulimia, it stems from a negative view they have of themselves, either physically or emotionally or both. Eating disorders are most common in the lives of teenage girls. That isn't too surprising, especially considering the issues of self-esteem that every single teenager has to face.

In addition, today's society puts great pressure on girls in particular to look a certain way. Add to these two factors the devil's lies, and the sum total is trouble.

According to God's Word, He made you, forming you in your mother's womb. First Corinthians 3:16 says that your body is the temple of the Holy Spirit. That means you are beautiful to God.

***You realize, don't you, that you are the temple of God, and God himself is present in you? No one will get by with vandalizing God's temple, you can be sure of that. God's temple is sacred — and you, remember, are the temple. — 1 Corinthians 3:16,17* THE MESSAGE**

Don't listen to what the devil has to say about you. Listen to what God and His Word say. If you have been struggling with eating disorders, pray and believe God to heal you on the inside. Then find a good doctor to help you learn how to take care of your body in a way that glorifies God in you.

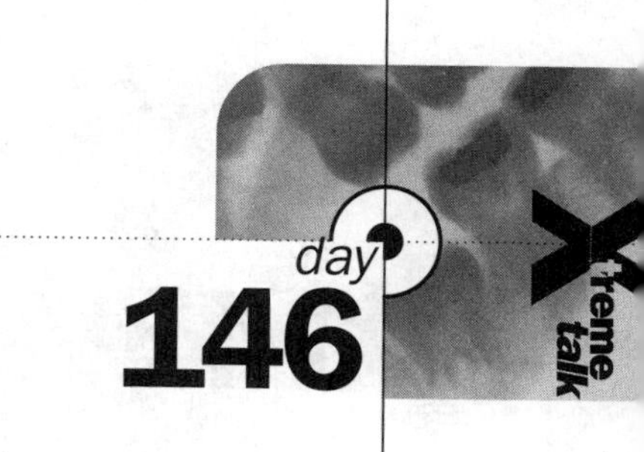

what is gluttony?

Gluttony is a subject that's hardly ever talked about. Gluttony basically means to overindulge your body with food or other sensual pleasures. Personally, I believe this problem can actually stem from attitudes and behavior in a person's teenage years.

The attitudes behind gluttony include selfishness, greed, lack of self-control and a lack of discipline. That's why Paul said that he made his body a slave. (1 Corinthians 9:27 NIV.) In other words, instead of letting his body rule *him,* Paul ruled *his body.*

What about you? Do you rule your body, or do you feed it as much as possible just because it tells you to?

Do not join those who drink too much wine or gorge themselves on meat, for drunkards and gluttons become poor, and drowsiness clothes them in rags. — Proverbs 23:20,21 NIV

If you exercise self-control and discipline now, it will be ingrained in you when your body needs it later on in life. Good habits start when you are young.

day
147

what is self-control, and how can I get it?

According to Galatians 5:22, self-control is a fruit of the Holy Spirit. But just because the Holy Spirit lives in us doesn't mean that we automatically have self-control. No, it's something that has to be *developed* on the inside of us.

This is how it works. First, the Holy Spirit prompts us to use self-control in a given situation. Then it is up to us to follow through and exercise it. Every time we choose to exercise self-control, that fruit of the Spirit grows stronger in our lives.

Self-control is a helpful quality to develop because it can benefit us in every part of our lives. As we practice self-control, we will begin to see the fruit of our efforts in every area of life.

But the fruit of the Spirit is love, joy, peace, patience, kindness, goodness, faithfulness, gentleness and self-control. Against such things there is no law. — Galatians 5:22,23 NIV

Are you letting your flesh rule you, or is the Holy Spirit in control of your life? Do you struggle with sexual indulgence, overeating or oversleeping? Make the decision to develop self-control. You *can* rule your body. Don't let *it* rule *you.*

I have always liked taking dares. do I have to stop now that I've become a Christian?

One of the most beautiful and possibly most dangerous attributes of teenagers is that they think they are invincible. If, however, a teenager turns this invincible confidence toward Christ, then look out, world — the devil is in trouble!

As a matter of fact, God is looking for people who are fearless to take on more risky assignments that need to be accomplished. He can take the love you have for adventure and use it to accomplish His purposes.

Think about the people who have smuggled Bibles into countries where Bibles aren't allowed or those who have been undercover missionaries in mainland China. God needs people who are out for adventure.

On the other hand, we shouldn't act foolishly, senselessly putting our lives at risk in order to impress others. If we do this, we may be stepping out from under the covering of God's protection and leading.

I like to think of it this way: God's protection over our lives is like a big umbrella. When we get caught in one of life's rainstorms, we had better stay under that umbrella. On the other hand, if we choose to go out from under God's protection, we can expect to get drenched.

A prudent man sees danger and takes refuge, but the simple keep going and suffer for it. — Proverbs 22:3 NIV

So use the common sense and wisdom God has already given you. Take responsibility for your life and the lives of others, and don't take foolish dares. Instead, refocus that desire for adventure by doing exploits for God!

is AIDS a disease that God sent to punish immoral people?

Let's set the record straight. AIDS is *not* a punishment sent by God for those He may deem as immoral. Sickness and disease are tools the enemy uses to destroy people. Unfortunately, he often convinces them to blame God for their tragedy. But nothing could be further from the truth.

***Don't overlook the obvious here, friends. With God, one day is as good as a thousand years, a thousand years as a day. God isn't late with his promise as some measure lateness. He is restraining himself on account of you, holding back the End because he doesn't want anyone lost. He's giving everyone space and time to change. — 2 Peter 3:8,9* THE MESSAGE**

God is a good God, and He wants more than anything for His people to experience a life free from the curse of the law, including the curse of sickness and death. In fact, Second Peter 3:9 says that it isn't God's will for *anybody* to perish. His desire is that all would come to Him with a repentant heart before it is too late. Nothing, not even a deadly disease such as AIDS, is too impossible for God to work through.

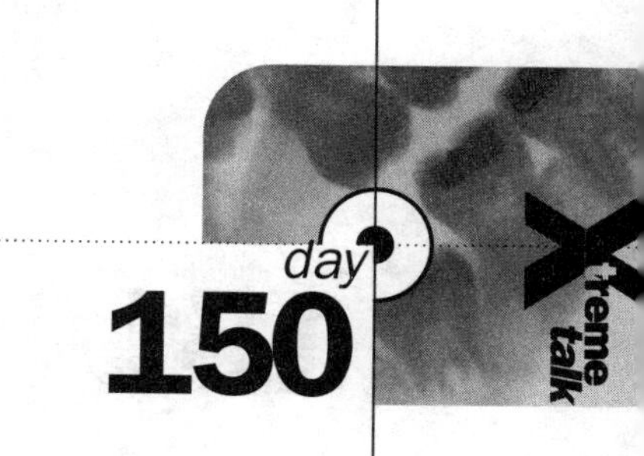

is there any way to stop worldwide hunger?

As a dad, I know how much it means to me that my children are healthy and provided for. Unfortunately, though, a lot of people get angry at God for things they believe are His fault, and that includes hunger and hopelessness. But don't be deceived; God wants every person to find security and health. It isn't His will for people to go around hungry and hurting.

As Christians, we all have the responsibility to spread the love of Christ to those who are hurting. We are the ones who should be feeding, clothing and praying for these hungry, hurting people.

Our Scriptures tell us that if you see your enemy hungry, go buy that person lunch, or if he's thirsty, get him a drink. Your generosity will surprise him with goodness. Don't let evil get the best of you; get the best of evil by doing good. — Romans 12:20,21 THE MESSAGE

I realize that at times the problem can seem overwhelming. But all we have to do is begin by helping just one person at a time. Then when the people we have helped hear God's message of love through us, they will be much more likely to come to the Lord because they will realize our words are backed up with actions.

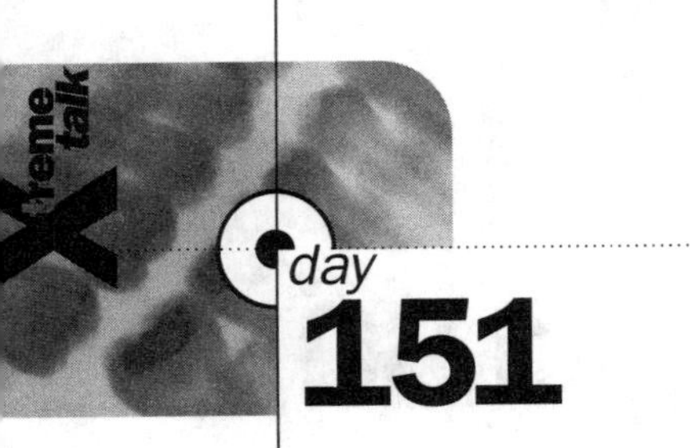

why is there so much suffering in the world today?

I know a lot of people have questions about all the suffering that's in the world and why it happens. They ask questions like: Why do wars happen? How can God allow human cruelty? What about all the injustices that happen?

Listen, the Lord is a just and loving Father. In fact, the Bible tells us in Romans 8 that nothing can separate us from His love.

God loves us so much that He wants us all to enjoy the blessings that are found in His Word. But He didn't create us to be robots, and He doesn't make our choices for us. And it is either our choices or the choices of other people that lead us into suffering.

For I am convinced that neither death nor life, neither angels nor demons, neither the present nor the future, nor any powers, neither height nor depth, nor anything else in all creation, will be able to separate us from the love of God that is in Christ Jesus our Lord. — Romans 8:38,39 NIV

The good news is that you are loved with an everlasting love and that God already has made a way for you to enjoy total peace and safety through Jesus Christ. The devil doesn't have to win. Through right choices, the Holy Spirit can help you beat the devil!

how important is showing compassion to others?

When the Bible talks about Jesus having compassion on other people, it always continues to tell us about an *action* that He took to help them.

In the same way, God's love requires us not just to *feel* the hurts of other people, but to *do* something about those hurts. After all, isn't that what God did for us when He sent His Son to die for us?

When they had finished eating, Jesus said to Simon Peter, "Simon son of John, do you truly love me more than these?" "Yes, Lord," he said, "you know that I love you." Jesus said, "Feed my lambs."

Again Jesus said, "Simon son of John, do you truly love me?" He answered, "Yes, Lord, you know that I love you." Jesus said, "Take care of my sheep."

The third time he said to him, "Simon son of John, do you love me?" Peter was hurt because Jesus asked him the third time, "Do you love me?" He said, "Lord, you know all things; you know that I love you." Jesus said, "Feed my sheep." — John 21:15-17 NIV

Every day you pass by people in need of God's love. Rather than walk by them with your good intentions intact, why don't you do something that could really make a difference in their lives? Jesus told Peter, "If you love Me, feed My lambs." (John 21:17.) Well, let that be His charge to you as well. Remember, compassion is an action!

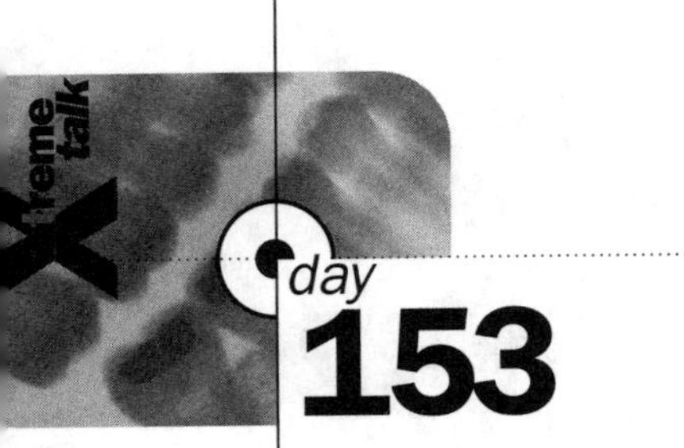

why is missions important?

Well, first of all, Jesus said, **Go ye into all the world, and preach the gospel to every creature** (Mark 16:15). Based on this verse and many others, it is evident that missions is a major part of God's heart. So whether you are called to send people or to go to the mission field yourself, missions is important.

One of the most impacting experiences I believe a young person could ever have is to take a missions trip. Not only will you have the opportunity to change nations for God, but you will be changed as well.

Personally, I know that my ministry experiences overseas have shaped who I am today. A new fire has been kindled in my heart for sharing Jesus with other people, and my boldness and compassion have increased.

Still later, as the Eleven were eating supper, he appeared and took them to task most severely for their stubborn unbelief, refusing to believe those who had seen him raised up. Then he said, "Go into the world. Go everywhere and announce the Message of God's good news to one and all. Whoever believes and is baptized is saved; whoever refuses to believe is damned." — Mark 16:15,16 THE MESSAGE

If you haven't already gone on a missions trip, pray about doing so. I assure you that it will transform you from the inside out.

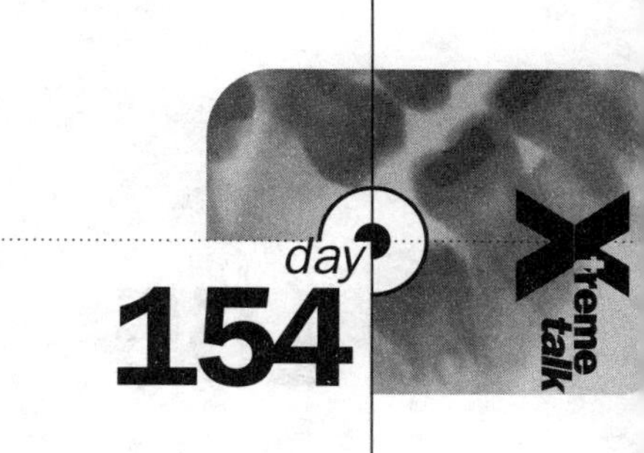

do spiritual truths bring you real happiness?

Whether or not people are Christians, most can quote John 8:32, which says that the truth shall set you free. But hold on a second. That isn't all that Scripture says. It actually says, **Ye shall *know* the truth, and the truth shall make you free.**

It isn't truth in itself that can do anything for you. Only when you know it and apply it to your life can you be set free.

Now, there are a lot of people who are searching for the truth. But few actually find it because the truth has become more gray than black and white.

That is why Jesus stands out as a clear solution. Unlike other so-called solutions, He is the Truth in a Person. When you accept Him and receive Him, He will teach you the truth and lead you into the truth in every area of your life.

And with each new revelation of the truth, you have the opportunity to make an adjustment. You don't have to become righteous based on your own effort. In fact, you *can't* become righteous by your own effort. That is why you need Christ. It is only through Him that you can really know how to change.

To the Jews who had believed him, Jesus said, "If you hold to my teaching, you are really my disciples. Then you will know the truth, and the truth will set you free." — John 8:31,32 NIV

When you know Christ, you know the Truth, and He sets you free. So determine to get to know Him today!

what is the best way to find yourself?

A lot of people talk about "finding themselves." They seem to think this will help them solve the problems they face in life. However, the problem usually isn't that they don't know themselves, but that their sin nature (or someone else's) has gotten in the way and caused a lot of problems.

Now don't get me wrong. I get excited when young people go on a search for their identity. It isn't necessarily bad. But the key to a successful search is the discovery of a void in their lives that can only be filled by God.

Everything of God gets expressed in him, so you can see and hear him clearly. You don't need a telescope, a microscope, or a horoscope to realize the fullness of Christ, and the emptiness of the universe without him. When you come to him, that fullness comes together for you, too. His power extends over everything.

Entering into this fullness is not something you figure out or achieve. No, you're already in — insiders.* — Colossians 2:9-11 *THE MESSAGE

Our true identity can only be found in Jesus Christ. Where we are lacking, He can make up the difference. The Bible puts it this way: "You are complete in Christ." (Colossians 2:10.)

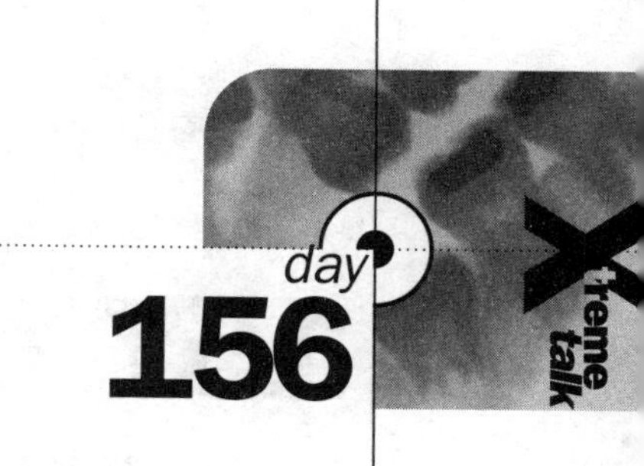

why are there so many false religions in the world today?

False religions are easy to spot because their viewpoints and traditions are contrary to the Word of God. They aren't based on Jesus Christ as our Sacrifice for sin. A false religion may acknowledge Jesus or some other main dude as a good teacher or an example worthy to be followed but not as a Savior.

Unfortunately, false religions are growing in popularity because so many people today are looking to the spiritual realm in order to find truth. Some find Jesus, but others are deceived into settling for a belief system that looks true without investigating the deception behind it.

Jesus said, "I am the Road, also the Truth, also the Life. No one gets to the Father apart from me. If you really knew me, you would know my Father as well. From now on, you do know him. You've even seen him!" — John 14:6,7 THE MESSAGE

People are looking for answers. Instead of letting them fall into a religion with just another good teacher as its centerpiece, why not give them the Answer to every spiritual need they have? Why not introduce them to Jesus Christ so they can have a relationship with God and not just with a dead religion?

day

157

how can people keep from believing in God when they look around at what He has created?

I have always had a hard time understanding atheism. To me, it takes a whole lot more faith to believe that there isn't a God than it does to believe there is One. In fact, Romans 1 talks about how all creation cries out that there is a Creator.

If you are reading this devotional and you are an atheist, I challenge you to study the intricacies of creation and then prove that there isn't a Supreme Being Who created it all. Remember, the more you know, the more you will find out that you don't know.

But God's angry displeasure erupts as acts of human mistrust and wrongdoing and lying accumulate, as people try to put a shroud over truth. But the basic reality of God is plain enough. Open your eyes and there it is! By taking a long and thoughtful look at what God has created, people have always been able to see what their eyes as such can't see: eternal power, for instance, and the mystery of his divine being. So nobody has a good excuse. — Romans 1:18-20 THE MESSAGE

Be open to the possibility that God exists. Forgive those who believe in God but may have hurt you in some way. God is bigger than your doubts and your hurts, and He will prove Himself to you because He is real.

does God really have a purpose for me to fulfill?

You are created for a specific purpose. The devil has used evolutionism and Darwinism to try to steal the idea of purpose from this generation. People who promote these theories try to convince us that just about everything we see in the world is a huge accident.

But understand this: It is no mistake that you have two eyes to see. It is no mistake that your heart leaps in you when you see someone you love. And it is no mistake that you have been put on this earth for such a time as this.

For you created my inmost being; you knit me together in my mother's womb. I praise you because I am fearfully and wonderfully made; your works are wonderful, I know that full well. My frame was not hidden from you when I was made in the secret place. When I was woven together in the depths of the earth, your eyes saw my unformed body. All the days ordained for me were written in your book before one of them came to be. — Psalm 139:13-16 NIV

Remember, God knew you before you were ever born. You are no surprise to Him, even if you were a surprise to your parents. You have been created for a purpose, and He will reveal it to you as you seek Him.

To receive Jesus as your Lord, pray this prayer...

Dear Heavenly Father,

I am so thankful that You love me so much. You sent Jesus to die on the cross for all of my sins. He paid the price for me so that I can receive complete forgiveness and have a pure relationship with You! I now receive Your salvation that has been made available to me.

I believe Jesus died on the cross for my sins and I confess Him as the Lord of my life. So according to Your Word, I AM SAVED! I am now Your child, forgiven and made complete in Christ. Thank You for forgiving my sins and giving me eternal life. In Jesus' Name, Amen.

Scripture References

John 3:16
1 John 1:7
Romans 5:8
Romans 10:13
Romans 10:9,10
Romans 8:15
Colossians 2:10
John 1:12
Ephesians 1:6

About the Author

Eastman Curtis is an internationally known speaker, author and television minister. He has reached hundreds of thousands through: his internationally aired television show "This Generation", 30 minute specials on many Fox affiliates, appearances on "700 Club" as a guest host, and a 60 second salvation commercial on MTV. Eastman has also produced several volumes of 90 second radio devotionals which have been enjoyed by audiences nationwide on over 500 stations for their practical and humorous teaching on real life issues.

Eastman travels the world preaching in churches, conferences, and ministry seminars, where he challenges teenagers and adults to fulfill God's destiny for their lives. He also hosts powerful, life-changing weekend crusades for young adults known as "This Generation Convention".

Eastman Curtis Ministries is located in Broken Arrow, OK, where they have recently started Destiny Church. This has fulfilled a dream that has been in their hearts for many years. Eastman and Angel live in Tulsa, Oklahoma where they are raising their son and daughter Sumner and Nicole.

To contact Eastman Curtis,
write:

Eastman Curtis
P. O. Box 470290
Tulsa, Oklahoma, 74147

Please include your prayer requests and comments when you write.

Other Books by Eastman Curtis

Dare to Destinize

Turn Loose of Your "But" and Go with God!

Kickin' Devil Hiney

Additional copies of this book
available from your local bookstore.

HARRISON HOUSE
Tulsa, Oklahoma 74153

The Harrison House Vision

Proclaiming the truth and the power
Of the Gospel of Jesus Christ
With excellence;
Challenging Christians to
Live victoriously,
Grow spiritually,
Know God intimately.